Backyard Vacation

Backyard Vacation

Outdoor Fun in Your Own Neighborhood

by
Carolyn Haas, Ann Cole, and Barbara Naftzger

Illustrated by Roland Rodegast

Little, Brown and Company
Boston   Toronto

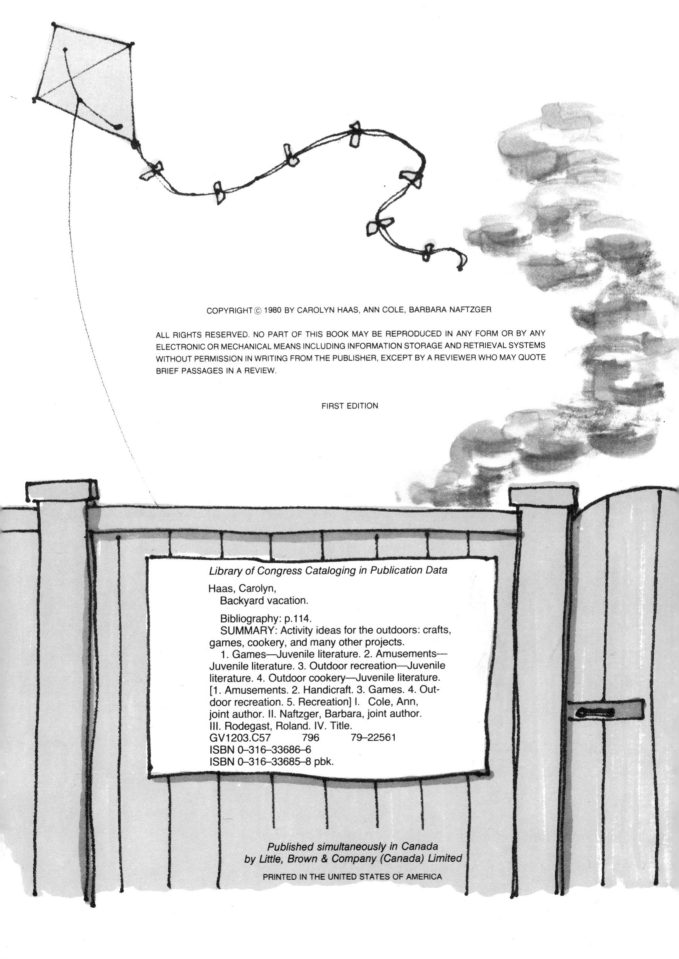

FIRST EDITION

Library of Congress Cataloging in Publication Data

Haas, Carolyn,
    Backyard vacation.

    Bibliography: p.114.
    SUMMARY: Activity ideas for the outdoors: crafts, games, cookery, and many other projects.
    1. Games—Juvenile literature. 2. Amusements—Juvenile literature. 3. Outdoor recreation—Juvenile literature. 4. Outdoor cookery—Juvenile literature. [1. Amusements. 2. Handicraft. 3. Games. 4. Outdoor recreation. 5. Recreation] I.   Cole, Ann, joint author. II. Naftzger, Barbara, joint author. III. Rodegast, Roland. IV. Title.
GV1203.C57   796   79–22561
ISBN 0–316–33686–6
ISBN 0–316–33685–8 pbk.

Published simultaneously in Canada
by Little, Brown & Company (Canada) Limited

PRINTED IN THE UNITED STATES OF AMERICA

To our husbands,
Bob Haas and Roger Cole,
and our children still at home:
Nancy, Laurie, and Danny Cole,
David, Susan, and Steve Naftzger,
who gave up dozens of hot dinners on cold snowy nights
during the winters of '78 and '79

Also by Carolyn Haas and Ann Cole

I SAW A PURPLE COW
And 100 Other Recipes for Learning
(with Faith Bushnell and Betty Weinberger)

A PUMPKIN IN A PEAR TREE
Creative Ideas for Twelve Months of Holiday Fun
(with Elizabeth Heller and Betty Weinberger)

CHILDREN ARE CHILDREN ARE CHILDREN
An Activity Approach to Exploring Brazil,
France, Iran, Japan, Nigeria and the U.S.S.R.
(with Betty Weinberger)

Contents

ACKNOWLEDGMENTS

We would like to thank the many people who helped us research and test out the projects in this book. These include our own children, as well as other kids in the neighborhood, authors, librarians, carpenters, architects, park district personnel, and craft and nature experts.

Special thanks go to our friends: Betty Weinberger, who helped us with the original concept, and Irene Feltes, our sounding board and typist; Gary Cole, Frisbee expert; Robert Corrigan, an award-winning high school architecture student; the late master carpenter Ralph Barenbrugge; architect Ray Johnson; tree specialist and naturalist Ralph Lee; bird expert Flo Sanders; nature and "whimmydiddle" expert Everett Sentman; and especially our editor and friend, John Keller, who saved the day!

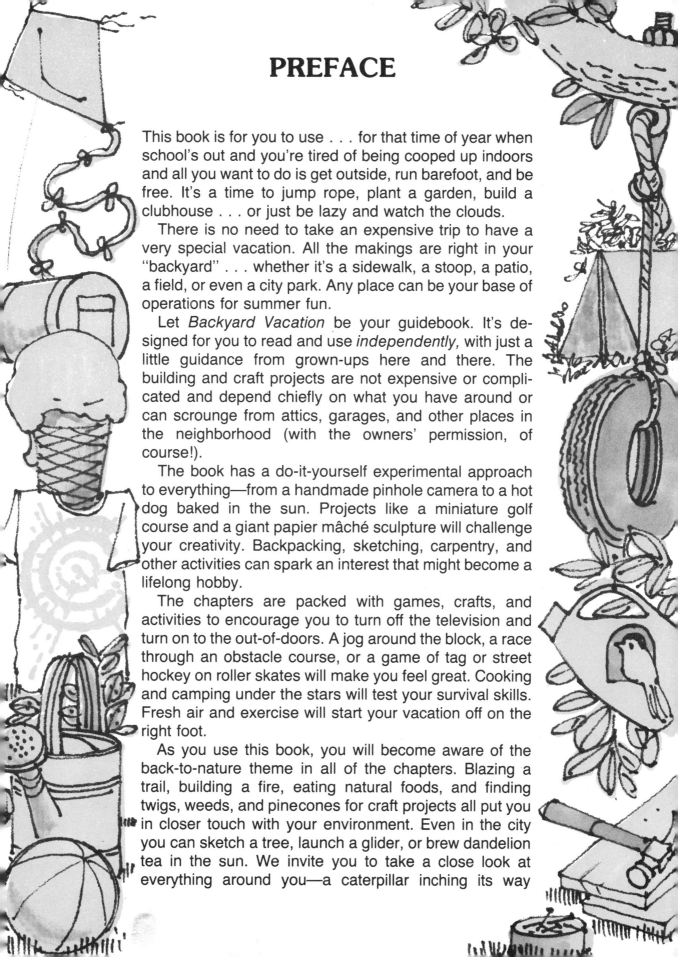

PREFACE

This book is for you to use . . . for that time of year when school's out and you're tired of being cooped up indoors and all you want to do is get outside, run barefoot, and be free. It's a time to jump rope, plant a garden, build a clubhouse . . . or just be lazy and watch the clouds.

There is no need to take an expensive trip to have a very special vacation. All the makings are right in your "backyard" . . . whether it's a sidewalk, a stoop, a patio, a field, or even a city park. Any place can be your base of operations for summer fun.

Let *Backyard Vacation* be your guidebook. It's designed for you to read and use *independently,* with just a little guidance from grown-ups here and there. The building and craft projects are not expensive or complicated and depend chiefly on what you have around or can scrounge from attics, garages, and other places in the neighborhood (with the owners' permission, of course!).

The book has a do-it-yourself experimental approach to everything—from a handmade pinhole camera to a hot dog baked in the sun. Projects like a miniature golf course and a giant papier mâché sculpture will challenge your creativity. Backpacking, sketching, carpentry, and other activities can spark an interest that might become a lifelong hobby.

The chapters are packed with games, crafts, and activities to encourage you to turn off the television and turn on to the out-of-doors. A jog around the block, a race through an obstacle course, or a game of tag or street hockey on roller skates will make you feel great. Cooking and camping under the stars will test your survival skills. Fresh air and exercise will start your vacation off on the right foot.

As you use this book, you will become aware of the back-to-nature theme in all of the chapters. Blazing a trail, building a fire, eating natural foods, and finding twigs, weeds, and pinecones for craft projects all put you in closer touch with your environment. Even in the city you can sketch a tree, launch a glider, or brew dandelion tea in the sun. We invite you to take a close look at everything around you—a caterpillar inching its way along a branch or a spider dangling from a newly spun silk thread—and to take time to hear a bird call when you go on an early morning walk.

Many of the ideas in *Backyard Vacation* are designed to get the whole neighborhood together. Parents and grandparents will enjoy an ice cream social or a country fair right along with you. There are even suggestions for fund raisers such as a bike shop, a flea market, and an art sale, where you can learn while you earn!

Whatever your age or interest, alone or with a crowd, there is something in this book for you. So pack your bags with imagination and energy and travel through these pages—your ticket for the best summer vacation yet!

Backyard Vacation

GETTING IT TOGETHER

Setting Up the Backyard

If you have a backyard, it will probably be your home base for many vacation-time activities. To set it up for a variety of games and projects, you may need to map out special areas. Find a sunny spot for a garden and a birdbath and a shady one for your pets. A work table will give you the space you need for craft, nature, and building projects, writing, painting, and picnicking. Scrounged materials—tires, lumber, utility spools, scrap pipes, bricks, wooden crates and barrels, and sturdy packing boxes, for example—are always handy. A homemade clubhouse can become a neighborhood center for your outdoor fun, especially on rainy days and after dark, too!

If you don't have a backyard, make the best use of whatever space you do have—porches, sides of buildings, front stoops, or even squares in the sidewalks. And don't forget a nearby playground, park, woods, or empty lot for exploring nature and other outdoor fun.

Building Projects

Making your own backyard equipment calls for certain basic tools. These include a hammer, saw, screwdriver, vise or clamps, hand drill, pliers, nails and screws, sandpaper, ruler, tape measure, and pencils. A large carton, a fishing tackle or lunch box, or even a bucket will make a handy carry-all for your supplies. (See pp. 17–20 for information on using various kinds of tools.)

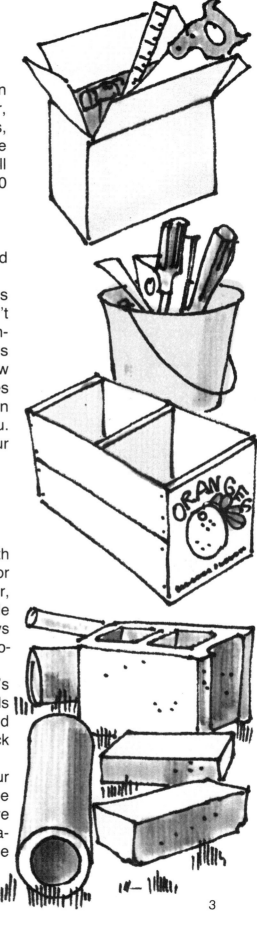

FINDING YOUR WOOD

First decide what you'd like to build and choose the wood that's right for the project.

You don't necessarily have to buy wood, since it is often available at building sites near you. But please don't help yourself—just ask the foreman for discards. Lumberyards usually have scrap boxes crammed full of odds and ends that you may get for free or for just a few dollars. Heavy wooden crates—the kind that vegetables and fruits are shipped in—are useful as is or can be taken apart for lumber. Ask your grocer to save these for you. Find out the best pickup time; then hitch a wagon to your bicycle for hauling away the wood.

TIPS FOR CARPENTRY

Safety First

1. Carpentry is often a cooperative effort, with some jobs requiring two or more people; for example, two people can haul the wood faster, and one person can hold the wood while another saws and hammers. However, always hammer a nail by yourself. This is not a two-person job!

2. For extra strength in any building project, it's best to use coated nails or *both* glue and nails because one will reinforce the other. Avoid Superglue, as it could make your fingers stick together too.

3. To prevent splinters, be sure you sand your wood well before building anything. But be careful; a really rough surface might have splinters that can go right through the sandpaper while you're working! Wrapping coarse sandpaper around a wood block will help.

3

4. Be careful when sawing not to cut the supporting table or workbench accidentally.
5. If your family has power tools and an adult will help you use them, they will save you some elbow grease and speed up the job considerably.
6. Remember, any time you use a saw, sawdust can get in your eyes. Protective glasses are an excellent precaution against both sawdust and flying wood chips.
7. A list of tools and materials and how to use them can be found beginning on p. 17. Choosing the right tools for the job and keeping them clean and in good repair will make you a better carpenter.

**SAFETY COMES FIRST
WHEN DOING CARPENTRY WORK.**

BALANCE BEAM

A balance beam is a good beginning carpentry project since it's easy to make and something you'll be using all summer long. Your younger brothers and sisters will enjoy walking across it too.

YOU NEED:

1 1 × 6 about 3 feet long* for the top
2 4 × 4 blocks of wood about 6 inches long for the supports
saw
hammer
nails (coated eightpenny with large heads)
sandpaper
stain

YOU DO:

1. Place a block of wood under each end of the 1 × 6 (or long board) and pound three nails through it into each wood block.
2. Sand and stain your balance beam before using it.

*If you want a longer balance beam, it's best to support it in the middle too.

CARPENTER'S SAWHORSE

Building a sawhorse from scratch can be a difficult job, but you'll be glad to have one (or two) to support your wood when you are making other things. Sawhorses also come in handy as props for many summer activities, like hurdles for an obstacle course or display tables for an art fair. It will be much easier to build one if you buy special sawhorse brackets at your local lumberyard or hardware store. (These cost anywhere from $3.00 to $6.00 a pair.) Then all you will have to do is cut the legs and top to size, or ask the lumberyard to do it for you. The legs will just slide into the brackets without needing to be *tapered*, which can be tricky.

YOU NEED:
1 2 × 4, 12 feet long (cut into 36-inch pieces) for the legs
1 2 × 4, 4 feet long for the top
nails (coated sixpenny)
sandpaper
stain
hammer
saw
brackets (one pair)
plywood and 1 × 2 boards for the shelf (optional)

YOU DO:
1. Cut the 12-foot board into four 36-inch pieces for the legs.
2. Slide two legs into each bracket and nail securely.
3. Stand up the legs, place your 2 × 4 over the top, and hammer several nails through it into each leg.
4. Sand your sawhorse and you'll be all set to take on more carpentry projects.

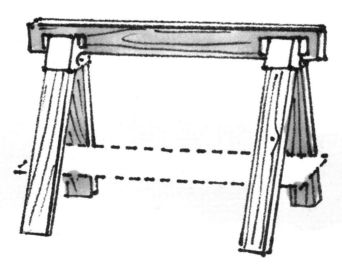

You might want to add a plywood *storage shelf* to the sawhorse, measuring it carefully to fit between the legs at a point about 10 inches above the ground.

TABLES AND STOOLS

A backyard table, besides being useful for a picnic, is handy for work projects and all sorts of play. Orange and milk crates or heavy wooden spools from a utility or wire company make sturdy tables. They come in various sizes and can be grouped together to fit whatever space you have.

Use smaller spools, crates, and barrels for stools. Nail kegs from the hardware store are just the right height.

If you want to make an all-purpose table, here is an easy way. Nail a piece of ¾-inch plywood or an old door onto two wooden boxes or two sawhorses. You might put a box on top or below your table to store supplies.

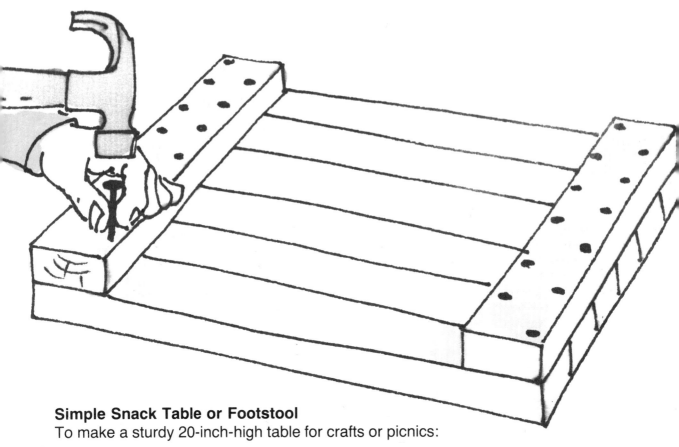

Simple Snack Table or Footstool

To make a sturdy 20-inch-high table for crafts or picnics:

YOU NEED:
3 2 × 4s, each 12 feet long
saw
square measure
sandpaper
nails (eightpenny)

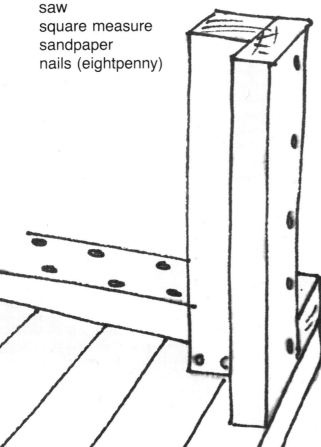

YOU DO:
1. For the table top, cut 2 of the 2 × 4 boards into 8 pieces, each 24 inches long.
2. Place 6 of them on the ground or any level surface. Then nail 2 pieces across each end to form the underside of the table top, as shown in the illustration.
3. For the legs, cut the 3rd board into 8 pieces, each 18 inches long. Nail pairs of boards together at right angles to make 4 "L"-shaped pieces.
4. Nail each leg in place at corners. (See illustration.)
5. Now turn your table over, sand well, and stain, if you wish.

Note: If you'd like to build a longer table, buy another 2 × 4 so you can make the 6 top boards longer.

STILTS

Stilts are great fun to walk on and not too hard to make.

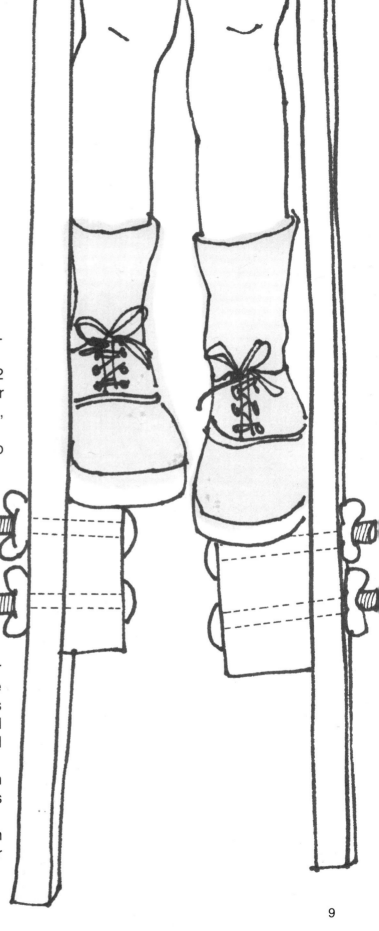

YOU NEED:

2 long boards (1½ × 2 inches) shoulder high for the poles

2 short pieces of wood roughly 2 inches wide and 4 inches long for foot rests (these can be triangles, squares, or rectangles)

4 wing nuts and 4 bolts long enough to go through the footrests and poles

hand drill

screwdriver

tape measure

pliers

pencil

YOU DO:

1. Decide what height you want your foot rests to be (a foot above the ground is about right) and mark this on the poles with a pencil. Then drill the holes. An extra set of holes will make your stilts adjustable.

2. Mark and drill two holes through each foot rest the same width as those on the poles.

3. Insert the bolts and secure with wing nuts using a pliers or your thumb and forefinger.

9

Tin Can Stilts

You can make a really simple pair of stilts out of two 48-ounce juice cans. Use a hammer and nail to punch 2 holes opposite each other near the closed end of each can. Then attach a piece of heavy twine or rope (about 6 feet long) to each can for a handle. Pull the rope taut as you step forward so the stilts will stick to your feet.

Once you're "off the ground," try some relays, a follow-the-leader game, or have a giraffe banquet . . . nibbling on a carrot, a celery stalk, or a doughnut hanging from a clothesline or tree branch!

RECYCLED WHEELS
There are lots of ways to "get rolling"! Just put pieces of scrap lumber together with some stray wheels and axles you've dug up. An old roller skate, golf cart, buggy frame, skateboard, or even some wheels from your little brother or sister's outgrown tricycle or go-cart will do just fine.

Roller Skate Scooter
Scooter riding has always been a favorite activity. You can put an old roller skate to good use by making a homemade scooter.

YOU NEED:
2 2 × 4s (each 3 feet long) or similar pieces of wood
2 1 × 2s for braces (12 inches each)
wood or a dowel for a handle (12 inches)
wood screws (1 inch and 2 inch) and washers
hammer
drill
screwdriver
bolts and nails (tenpenny)

YOU DO:
1. Drill a hole 1 inch deep on the underside of one 2 × 4. Then attach a pair of wheels into one of the 2 × 4s. Use the hole in the skate for your nail or screw.
2. Join the base and the other 2 × 4 with wood screws to make an "L."
3. Nail the 1 × 2s across the "L" to brace your scooter (or cut out a triangular piece of wood for an even stronger support).
4. Drill two holes big enough for 2-inch screws through the dowel and attach the handle.

Scooterboard

Put furniture casters or a pair of roller-skate wheels on each corner of a piece of board or plywood that is about ½ inch thick and 16 to 18 inches long. Then lie down on the board and push with your feet; or get on your hands and knees and push with one foot. It's fun however you do it, but be safe and don't stand up on it.

WHEN YOU'RE ON WHEELS,

STAY ON THE SIDEWALK

AND OFF BUSY STREETS

AND STEEP HILLS.

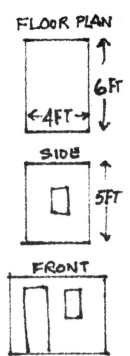

FLOOR PLAN

6 FT

←4FT→

SIDE

5FT

FRONT

CLUBHOUSE

Probably the most challenging construction project for the backyard is a clubhouse, a special meeting place for you and your friends and NO ADULTS ALLOWED! You can make it into a fort, a pioneer cabin, a cave, or a castle—or anything else you might dream up!

It's fun to create a clubhouse out of all kinds of scrap lumber, letting your imagination guide your hammer, but if you'd like to build a really sturdy house, here is how you might go about it.

First decide what size to make your house. Then draw a floor plan showing the length, width, and height. Ask your parents or call city hall to find out about local zoning laws (the rules for building in your area) before you begin this project.

Here's a sample clubhouse that's not too hard to make.

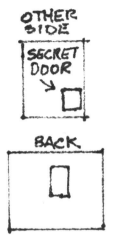

OTHER SIDE

SECRET DOOR →

BACK

The Basic Platform

YOU NEED:

3 beams of the same length for support
  (2 × 4s about 6 feet long are good)
boards or a piece of plywood cut to the
  size you have chosen
lots of 1⅞-inch (fivepenny) nails
hammer
tape measure
glue

YOU DO:

1. Lay the beams down on the ground, placing one at each end and one in the middle, following your floor plan.
2. Starting at one end, lay one board across the beams, and hammer two nails through it into each beam. Continue in this fashion until all of the boards are securely attached.

Sides and Roof
YOU NEED:

4 posts (2 × 4s or 4 × 4s) for supports

pieces of plywood, scrap wood, or planks for sides and roof

saw

hammer

nails, 1⅞-inch (fivepenny)

tape measure

pencil

YOU DO:

1. Stand up with your arms stretched over your head, and have a friend measure the distance from the ground to your fingertips. Then you'll know how high to cut the posts of your clubhouse. (This will give you growing room!)
2. Cut your wood for the sides and roof according to your diagram.
3. To make the first side, lay two of the posts on the ground and nail your cut wood or scrap lumber into them. Do the same thing for the opposite side.
4. With the help of your friends, nail each side into your basic platform.
5. Now nail wood to the posts to make the back and front of your house. Leave spaces for a door and windows. (If using plywood, saw these out.)
6. Finally, you are ready to nail the roof into place. (Use a large sheet of plywood or build it as you did the walls.)

If you decide to turn your clubhouse into a tree house, be sure to get an adult's help. It's sometimes hard to build something safe and sturdy in a tree, unless you're a bird!

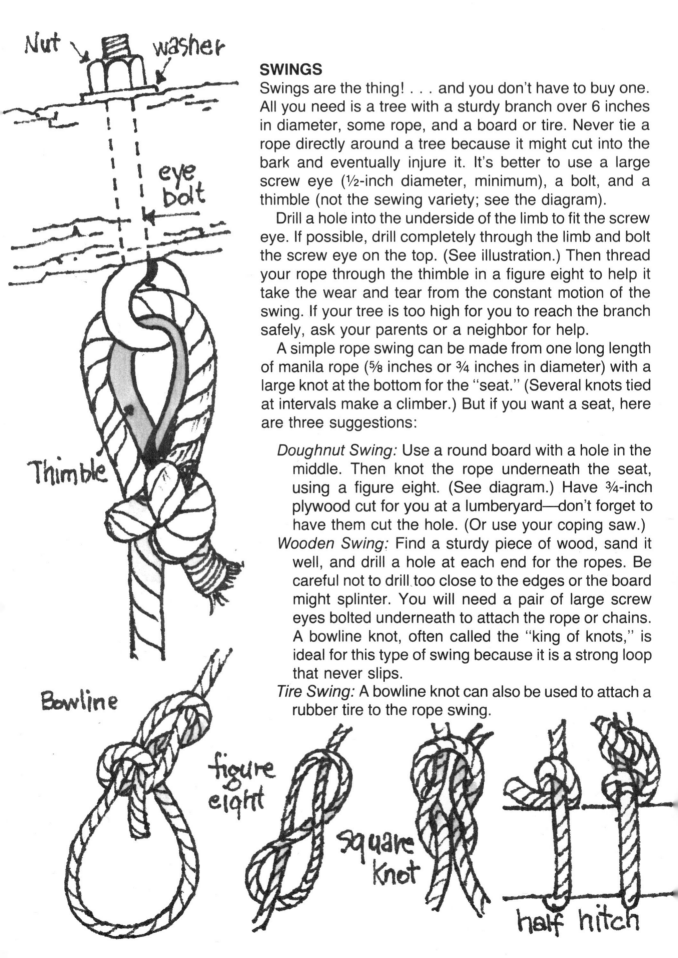

Nut **washer**

eye bolt

Thimble

Bowline

figure eight

square knot

half hitch

SWINGS

Swings are the thing! . . . and you don't have to buy one. All you need is a tree with a sturdy branch over 6 inches in diameter, some rope, and a board or tire. Never tie a rope directly around a tree because it might cut into the bark and eventually injure it. It's better to use a large screw eye (½-inch diameter, minimum), a bolt, and a thimble (not the sewing variety; see the diagram).

Drill a hole into the underside of the limb to fit the screw eye. If possible, drill completely through the limb and bolt the screw eye on the top. (See illustration.) Then thread your rope through the thimble in a figure eight to help it take the wear and tear from the constant motion of the swing. If your tree is too high for you to reach the branch safely, ask your parents or a neighbor for help.

A simple rope swing can be made from one long length of manila rope (⅝ inches or ¾ inches in diameter) with a large knot at the bottom for the "seat." (Several knots tied at intervals make a climber.) But if you want a seat, here are three suggestions:

Doughnut Swing: Use a round board with a hole in the middle. Then knot the rope underneath the seat, using a figure eight. (See diagram.) Have ¾-inch plywood cut for you at a lumberyard—don't forget to have them cut the hole. (Or use your coping saw.)

Wooden Swing: Find a sturdy piece of wood, sand it well, and drill a hole at each end for the ropes. Be careful not to drill too close to the edges or the board might splinter. You will need a pair of large screw eyes bolted underneath to attach the rope or chains. A bowline knot, often called the "king of knots," is ideal for this type of swing because it is a strong loop that never slips.

Tire Swing: A bowline knot can also be used to attach a rubber tire to the rope swing.

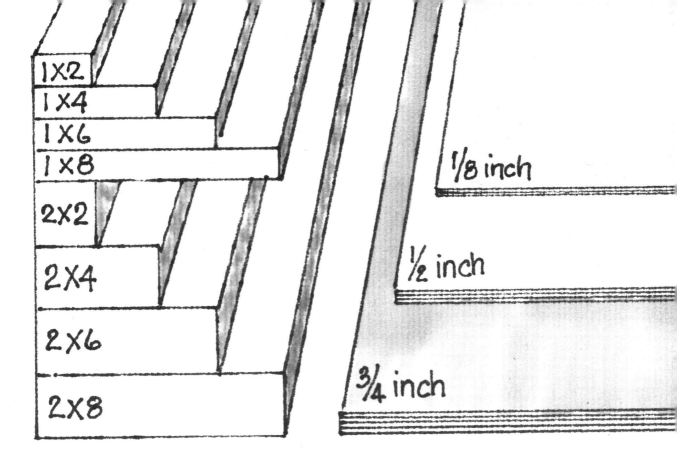

1X2
1 X4
1 X6
1 X8
2X2
2X4
2X6
2X8

1/8 inch
1/2 inch
3/4 inch

Materials, Tools, and Techniques

WOOD

Soft wood, such as pine, is the easiest kind for building. To make it last longer outdoors, brush on a sealer or a varnish. You might also want to paint or stain your wood. Redwood and cedar, although expensive, are ideal for outside projects because they last longer than untreated woods.

Plywood, useful for building large areas like roofs, walls, and floors, is made of narrow layers of wood pressed together. It comes in various thicknesses (⅛ inch to ¾ inch) and is stocked in 4-foot by 8-foot sheets. For a small charge, the lumberyard will cut it to size. Plywood is graded *interior* and *exterior,* as well as *A,B,C,* and *D,* with *A* having the smoothest surface on both sides. The exterior grade costs more but is better suited to your outdoor projects.

Boards come in various stock sizes: 1-inch stock (1 × 2, 1 × 4, 1 × 6, 1 × 8, etc.) and 2-inch stock (2 × 2, 2 × 4, etc.). The second number tells you how wide the board is.

HAMMER AND NAILS

Nails come in many different lengths and thicknesses, twopenny to tenpenny (abbreviated 2d to 10d).* Four-penny to eightpenny are the sizes for projects in this book. The higher the number, the bigger the nail. Nails with large heads and coated with resin (a gummy substance from pine and fir trees) work well for most projects because the resin will melt and stick to the wood like glue.

Choose a nail a half-inch shorter than the combined thickness of the two pieces to be joined so it won't poke through the wood. To keep the wood from splitting, a good rule of thumb is: the thinner the wood, the thinner the nail. Drill a small hole first where you're going to pound in the nail.

Use a full-size, but lightweight hammer. Avoid the inexpensive ones that tend to break easily. When you hammer in a nail, hold the hammer firmly and try to hit the nail squarely on the head, tapping a few times at first until it takes hold. Hammer your nails in as straight as possible.

*In case you're wondering where the *penny* comes from, it meant how much 100 nails cost—hence, the bigger the nail, the bigger the penny number.

SAWS

Sawing is hard work and should be done with care; however, a sharp saw will make your work easier. It's best to buy an all-purpose, crosscut handsaw about 26 inches in length. A coping saw with a thin, narrow blade that can cut inside shapes is also useful. You will need several interchangeable blades.

To support the wood you are sawing, lay it down on a sawhorse or two, a workbench, a table, a step stool, or a tree stump, with the part to be sawn off extending over the edge. Use a vise or C-clamp to hold your wood steady. Draw a line where you want to cut, then saw away in a slow, even rhythm. Save the sawdust in a bag or box for later craft projects.

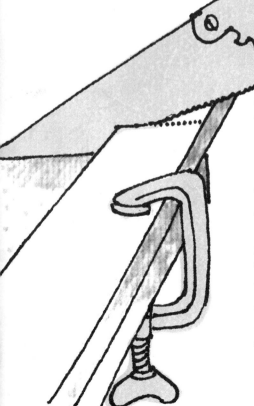

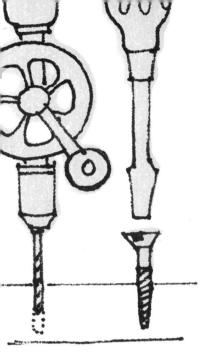

HAND DRILL AND SCREWS

When wood is joined together with screws rather than nails, it is less likely to pull apart. A drill is fitted with "bits" (thin steel rods of different sizes that are turned by the handle) to make holes for the screws. Mark the place where you want to drill your hole. Choose wood screws a little shorter than the thickness of the wood, and a bit slightly smaller than your screw. Screwdrivers come in different sizes to match the grooves in the heads of the screws. Two screwdrivers with 3/16 and 5/16 blades should be all you need.

SANDPAPER

Sandpaper is sold in sheets, from a fine to a coarse grade. A medium sandpaper will work well for most building projects. Cut a sheet into quarters and wrap one of these around a piece of scrap lumber for sanding flat surfaces. It is usually best to sand your wood after your project is completed unless it is very rough and might cause splinters. Sand with the grain (following the lines of the wood) except at the ends, where you sand across the grain.

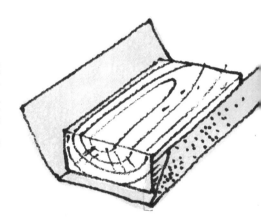

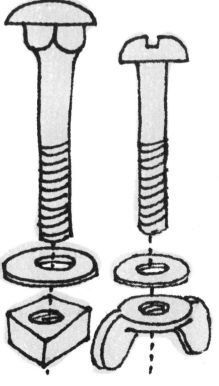

NUTS, BOLTS, AND WASHERS

Bolts are used to fasten objects together, and nuts fit at the ends of the bolts to keep them tight and in place. For the projects in this book, you will need bolts from ⅛ inch to ⅜ inch in diameter and from 1 inch to 3 inches long. Square nuts are used on permanent attachments and need to be tightened with a wrench. A washer is a round metal disc with a hole in the center that is used between the nut and wood to keep the bolt from slipping. For wing nuts that you might want to remove from time to time, use pliers or your forefinger and thumb.

STAIN, PAINT, AND VARNISH

Before buying any paints or stains, read all of the labels carefully so you can select the *right* cleaning solution. Ask a salesperson to advise you on the type of brush that is best for the paint or stain. There are many products to color and seal wood. Stain, even though it is thin, will protect wood and give it a light or dark tone, depending on which one you choose—oak, pine, walnut, etc. Paint, especially *exterior latex,* is thicker than stain and will be more durable. Latex paint can be washed off with soap and water if it spills on you, your clothes, or anything else. Cleaning the brushes is also easy with latex paint. Oil-based paint is harder to clean up, since you must use turpentine or paint thinner.

Varnish and shellac are clear finishes that are brushed or sprayed on painted or stained wood as a protective sealer. Varnish is oil-based and usually glossy, requiring turpentine for cleaning brushes and any drips. Shellac is similar to varnish but is alcohol-based, so denatured alcohol is needed for cleaning up. For a professional finish, put on a coat of varnish or shellac, let it dry, sand it, and add another coat. Be sure the paint or stain is *dry* before putting on any of these finishes.

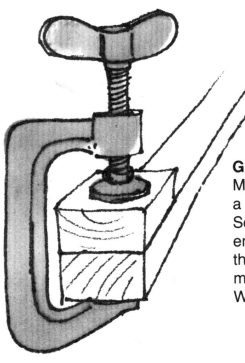

GLUE

Many smaller carpentry projects can be made using just a white water-based glue. Elmer's Glue All, Tightbond, Sobo, and other brands will bond wood together permanently. Apply the glue at places you have marked and hold the two pieces together for a few minutes (or use masking tape or clamps to keep the pieces in place). Wipe off excess glue, and let it set overnight.

LETTING OFF STEAM

Fun and Games with Water

WATER SLIDE

On those hot summer days, a water slide will provide cool, slippery fun. All you need is a length of heavy plastic (five or six yards long), some smooth rocks to hold it down (if necessary), and a bucket of water or a hose. You can buy strong plastic runners or sheeting at a discount store or fabric center.

Find a grassy place, unroll your slide, and turn on the hose (or throw on a bucket of water). Then get a running start and ZOOM—you'll be slipping and sliding in all directions!

See who can go the entire length without stopping. Play Follow the Leader and invent other games. Try using large plastic lids, platters, ice cube trays, or even a Frisbee as sleds.

Be sure to keep the surface of the slide wet and move it around often so that the *grass won't get brown.* When you're worn out, pick up your slide and hang it up to dry for use on another hot day.

21

HULA HOOP SPRINKLER

Try putting together this unique circular sprinkler.

YOU NEED:
1 hula hoop
1 hose
1 PVC fitting (plumbing fixture that joins two open hose ends together)
washer (to keep water from leaking)
hose connector
hammer
long nail

YOU DO:
1. With a hammer and nail, punch holes all around one side of the hula hoop, about 1 or 2 inches apart, being careful not to hammer through to the underside.
2. Cut through the hoop and attach each open end to the PVC fitting. (See illustration.)
3. Hook it up to your garden hose, and you'll be all set for hours of fun.

Can you figure out a way to hang the hoop upside down to make an outdoor shower?

WATER GAMES

Another way to beat the heat is with a squirt gun or water balloons. Fill balloons with water directly from the hose or from a bucket and tie a knot at the end. Gather up your "ammunition," and then fire away . . . the battle is on!

Try another game with your water balloons. Toss one to a friend, beginning up close together and taking a step backward after each throw. How far apart can you get before somebody gets soaked?

BUBBLE MANIA

You can blow zillions of bubbles by experimenting with dippers or wands made from rubber bands, plastic drinking straws with the ends split, plastic six-pack holders, cans with both ends cut out, and paper clips bent into various shapes.

Here's a recipe for bubble mix:

½ cup liquid detergent to 1 quart of water

If you add ⅓ to ½ cup of glycerine and a pinch of sugar to your bubble water, you can create giant bubbles that will hold their shape longer than the usual soap-and-water variety. Glycerine is available at most drugstores, but is expensive.

Make a giant bubble blower out of a coat hanger, an embroidery hoop, or an old foil pie pan with the center cut out. Just dip it in the bubble mix and swirl it around. The record for the biggest bubble ever is said to be ten inches across. Can you beat that?

Electric Bubbles

Would you like to make a static-electric bubble? Bend the end of a copper wire into a circle or loop, and catch a bubble on top of it. Then run a comb across your hair or against some wool to "charge it up," and bring it close to the bubble. Now see how the bubble twists into all sorts of shapes.

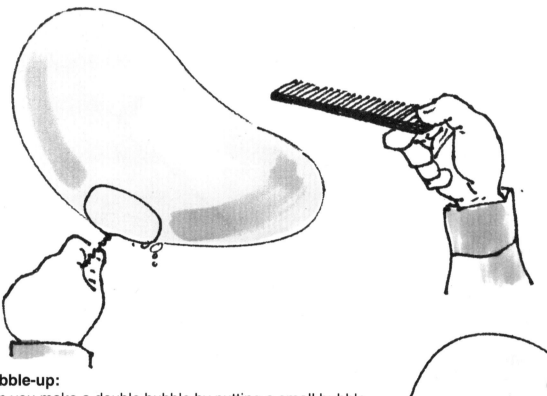

Bubble-up:

Can you make a double bubble by putting a small bubble inside a larger one? Dip your wand into the mixture to make one bubble. Then dip it in again and pick up a larger bubble. What happens when you experiment with different amounts of glycerine or food coloring in your bubble mix? Can you make a tricolored bubble? Quickly dip your loop into three different colors, or try making a "chain" by connecting three bubbles of different colors.

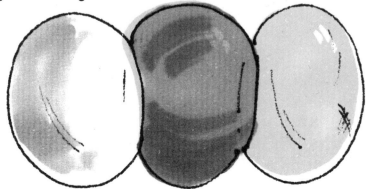

Obstacle Course

OVER

UNDER

THROUGH

JUMP
1.
2.
3.

SWING

You can set up this challenging activity in your own yard or at a nearby park or playground using equipment that you've brought with you, as well as slides, swings, or whatever is already there. Collect all kinds of things from your yard, garage, or basement, or scrounge around the neighborhood for castoffs: for example, a bucket, a broom, old tires, a barrel, a three-legged stool, planks, bricks, a ball.

First set up a course that calls for a variety of skills. Be sure they are challenging enough for kids of your age. You'll want to include running, jumping, climbing, balancing, throwing, and catching. Some ideas for activities are: crawling through a barrel; hopping in and out of a tire or a whole line of them; shinnying up a pole or rope; throwing a ball into a bucket or basket or over a tree limb and catching it on the other side; walking along a narrow plank set on two bricks; or jumping over a box or pile of leaves or newspapers.

Have each person "test run" the course several times from start to finish to become familiar with the layout. Then using a stopwatch or kitchen timer, you can run through the obstacles, trying to better your own time, race against each to see who is the fastest, or if you like, set up team competition.

If you find yourself doing a lot of huffing and puffing while going through the course, maybe you need to exercise more.

OVER

FINISH

THROUGH

HOP ON ONE FOOT

Getting in Shape

Exercising makes you feel great and it's fun. Experts consider the kind of exercises called *aerobic* (walking, running, cycling, swimming, skipping rope, and cross-country skiing) to be the best kind because they help you use oxygen more efficiently. But before you begin, here are some good rules to know.

Commonsense Rules for Doing Any Exercise
1. Exercise regularly—every day, if possible, or at least three or four times a week.
2. Dress for comfort. Wear loose clothing and lightweight, flexible track shoes that are cushioned for running.
3. Avoid doing strenuous exercises after you have eaten a large meal.
4. Be sure to warm up first with a few basic exercises like arm circles and leg swings.
5. Don't overdo. Begin slowly with just a few exercises at a time.
6. Drink lots of liquids afterward (when you have cooled down) to replace what you've lost in perspiration.

What rules would you add to this list?

FITNESS TRAIL

Set up an exercise course with "stops" (called *fitness stations*) along the way to practice some aerobics. Just as you did with the obstacle course, you can test your skills by yourself alone or with a group. You could even use several backyards, or stake out a trail on the sidewalk, an alley, a nearby playing field, or a vacant lot. Mark your course with signs describing the exercise to be done at each stop. Whatever exercise you choose will help you become stronger and have better balance, endurance, and coordination. Here are some examples of the exercises you could do at each station.

Station 1: Warm-ups

Football and soccer players like to use these exercises to limber up:

Arm Circles: Keeping your elbows straight and your palms up, begin by making small clockwise circles; then gradually make bigger and bigger arcs. Repeat, making backward circles.

Leg Swings: Standing erect, swing one leg forward and back several times and then out to the side. Repeat with the other leg.

Touch your toes and do some sit-ups, push-ups, and jumping jacks or other stretching and bending exercises.

Station 2: Tumbling

All you need at this station is an exercise mat. You can use an old mattress, some blankets or quilts folded in half, or a length of polyurethane padding. You could also buy an inexpensive mat at a drugstore or sporting goods store.

Start with forward and backward rolls and, depending on your ability, advance to stunts like cartwheels and handstands. People stationed at either side of the mat will help the tumblers do their tricks and keep them from falling. You might even enjoy doing your tumbling routines to music or to the beat of a drum to help you keep the rhythm.

The *monkey roll* takes three people and is really a challenge! With hands and knees on the mat, line up, all facing the same direction. The one in the middle rolls to the right while the person on the right dives over him and continues rolling to the lefthand position; then the person originally on the left dives over him, landing in the middle. Repeat as many times as you like.

Station 3: Jumping Rope

Many coaches think that jumping rope is the perfect exercise. Athletes get in shape with a jump rope, and you can, too. Jump on one foot, then the other, forward and backward, fast and slow . . . the possibilities are endless. Here are two jingles to keep you going. More can be found on p. 47. Now start counting . . .

Ice Cream Soda
Ice cream, soda water, gingerale, pop,
How many times can you hop, hop, hop?
1–2–3–4 . . .

Measles, Mumps
Measles, mumps
Little red bumps.
Doctor's needles
In our rumps.
Little David really jumps.
Ouch, 2, 3, 4, 5, 6 . . .

How long can you last at this station?

Station 4: Jogging

When you get to this stop, it's time to jog around your yard or neighborhood. Map out a course of about a mile and see how fast you can go. Beginning joggers should start slowly and increase their speed and distance gradually. When you get tired, alternate walking and running. If you can run a mile in eight to ten minutes, you are physically fit!

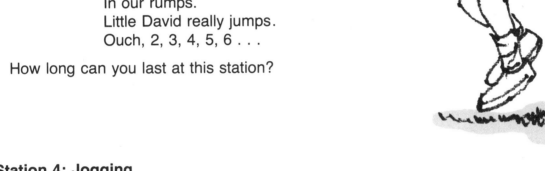

You and your friends might enjoy having your own "jog log." Just write down your miles in a notebook or punch out each mile on a card. How about starting a hundred-mile club? Everyone who has run a hundred miles can join. But why stop there? Use your jogging course to "run" across the United States! You'd probably find the 2,786 miles from New York City to Los Angeles a bit exhausting, but you could start from your own home town and choose a nearby city for your "final destination." Keep track of your progress by marking off your miles on a map each week. This is a journey that could take all summer!

Junior Olympics

Have fun with your neighborhood gang and keep physically fit at the same time. Organize an Olympics on your street that can be a one-day event or last the entire week.

Get together to plan the athletic events for the competition. These might include:

- balance beam (planks across two bricks or wood blocks, or a row of bricks, or use your homemade one)
- high jump (broomstick resting on a pair of bricks, overturned buckets, or stools)
- ball throw (beach or soccer ball)
- spear throwing (a yardstick or branch)
- discus throw (Frisbee toss for distance)
- sit-ups, push-ups, toe touches (the number you can do in one minute)
- broad jump (standing or running)
- floor exercises (dancing and gymnastics to a drumbeat or tape recorder, or music on your portable radio)
- marathon run (10 times around the block)

A week before the Olympics, post sign-up sheets around the neighborhood listing each event, with space for the athletes' names. Try to have at least four people entered in each category. Who will be brave enough to sign up for the marathon race? Make up a list of all the equipment needed, including a stopwatch, so you'll have everything ready.

Make "medals" for the winners by cutting cardboard circles and covering them with gold, silver, and bronze paint or paper for first, second, and third prize. Punch a hole at the top for yarn or ribbon to place over the heads of the award-winning athletes.

You'll probably need a giant poster to use as an official scoreboard so that the points for each event can be tallied at the end of the competition.

For the reviewing stand, decorate the porch or stoop with colorful streamers and set up chairs and a table for the judges. Schedule one event at a time and take turns being a judge so everyone can participate.

Finally, you're ready to begin. With all of the spectators and athletes eagerly waiting, welcome the "herald" waving his "flaming" torch as he runs through the crowd. The Olympic Games are on!

OUTDOOR GAMES

Games, games, and more games . . . from the earliest times, kids all over the world have enjoyed playing games. They can be played almost anywhere—in a park or playground, on a sidewalk, or on a quiet street—whatever space you use as your "backyard." Be inventive. Use whatever equipment you have around (or make your own) and set ground rules that are fair to everyone.

Get a Gang Together— Nothing Else Required

Some old-time favorites everyone probably knows are Hide and Seek, Red Rover, Follow the Leader (you might use your obstacle course, p. 25, for this one), Red Light Green Light, Grandmother, May I? Statues, and, of course, many varieties of tag and relay games. Here are some that you may not know that are especially fun for groups to use on the spur of the moment.

CHAIN TAG
Whoever is "It" tries to catch the others, one by one. The first person caught joins hands with "It," and the two of them together chase the others, forming a chain and tagging from each end. The chain grows longer as each new "link" is added. Set boundaries to limit the size of the playing area and continue until everyone is part of the chain, or until time is called.

STOOP TAG, TV STYLE

The person who is tagged stoops and quickly gives the name of a TV show (or a movie star, an athlete, or some other category). If she can't come up with a name by the count of three, she becomes "It."

JOHNNY CAN'T CROSS THE OCEAN

This game is played on a street or wherever there is a fairly large space. All the players are on one side of the "ocean," with "It" standing in the middle between the players and the opposite "shore" (goal line). He calls out, "Johnny can't cross my ocean unless he has on the color—————" (names a color). Whoever is wearing that color shows it and gets to cross the "ocean" free. The rest then try to reach the opposite "shore" without being tagged. The game continues until all are caught. The last one left is "It" for the next game.

Variation: Instead of colors, you may want to use names beginning with different letters, birthdays in certain months, or anything else you want.

33

EXERCISE RELAY

Line up in teams behind a starting line. At the signal, the first person on each team runs to a spot and performs some sort of exercise (ten times or whatever the group decides)—for example, arm circles, toe touches, or jumping jacks. The rest of the team members copy the same exercise at the same time. The first players then run back to the end of their line and the second player in each line hurries to begin a *new* exercise for her team to copy.

CHARLIE CHAPLIN RELAY

Use your imagination to think up different ways of moving for this unusual relay. Here are some suggestions to get you started. How about running in slow motion like a videotape replay, walking sideways like a crab, clawing the air like a monster . . . or even imitating the jaunty walk of Charlie Chaplin? This is run like the usual relay with teams, everyone doing the *same* thing.

Here are a couple of togetherness games:

SARDINES
This is a form of Hide and Seek. The player who is "It" finds a hiding place, while the others count to a hundred before going to look for him. Each player who discovers the secret spot joins "It"—and soon everyone is squashed together in the same hiding place like sardines in a can. The last player left becomes "It" for the next round. This is fun to play at night with flashlights.

WHEELBARROW CRAM
After playing Sardines, you should be a real expert at this game. How many of you can cram into a wheelbarrow, fit under a table, or into your clubhouse, or anywhere else you choose? Try guessing the total number ahead of time and see who comes the closest.

ADD-A-NOISE

Sit in a circle and choose someone to make a sound—a cough, sigh, slurp, sneeze, whistle, snap, click, clap on the thigh . . . any noise will do. The next person repeats the sound, adding another one, and so on around the circle. Whoever forgets or gets the order confused is out and must sit in the soup (the middle of the circle).

SNAP

Decide on three different faces (happy, mean, silly, scary) and practice making them. Divide into pairs, turn back to back, and at a signal make one of the faces and turn around. If both have the *same* expression, the first one to call "snap" wins. If the faces are different, repeat until there is a "snap." This game can be played over and over, perhaps with winners playing winners and losers against losers . . . or "face off" winners of each twosome to find the Grand Snap Champ.

CRAZY CHARADES

Instead of the usual charades—movies, book titles, television shows, popular sayings—try acting out some silly scenes with a partner to see how quickly your team can guess what you are doing. Be sure to set a time limit first. Some suggestions to get you started are searching through a darkened movie theater for a friend; a mad scientist and her creation as it takes shape; a skier trying to go downhill backward; a tightrope walker with a broken leg. What crazy things can *you* think up?

Group Games—Some Equipment Needed

A few old-timers are Kick the Can, Steal the Bacon, Street Hockey, Capture the Flag, Jump the Brook, and Tug-o-War. Here are some you may not know.

ALL OR NOTHING BEAN BAG THROW

Here's a novel bean bag game where the winners take all! Like shuffleboard, it calls for four players, two to a team, and eight bean bags, four for each side. Players take turns throwing a bean bag into the target (can, tire, wastebasket, or a box with a hole cut in it), scoring a point for each hit . . . but there is a catch! The side that scores *last* gets all of the points and is the first one to throw the next time. For example, your opponent could score four times, but if you have the last turn and hit the target, you get all five points for that round.

Hint: An easy way to make a bean bag is to cut off the top of an old sock, fill it with beans, and sew it shut.

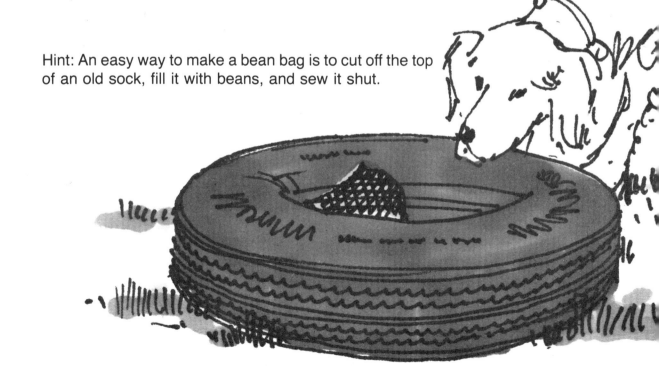

Here are some more relays, but these call for just a few materials.

SUITCASE RELAY

A suitcase for each team containing four or five items of oversized clothing (baggy trousers, long skirts, shirts, hats, high heels, necktie, work gloves, and anything else you can think of) is placed at the goal line. The first player on each team runs to the suitcase, opens it, and quickly puts on all of the clothes. He closes the suitcase, picks it up, and runs back to his team, where he takes off the clothes as quickly as he can with the help of the next player waiting in line. He then repacks the suitcase and hands it to his helper, who runs back to the goal line and repeats the action. You can play this game with just an oversized pullover sweater and forget the suitcase if you wish.

CHEWING GUM RELAY

Give each team a pack of sugarless chewing gum and a pair of gloves. The first person in line puts on the gloves, unwraps a stick of gum, and begins chewing. She then hands the gloves and the pack of gum to the next in line, who repeats the action until everyone on the team is chewing away. Bubble gum is even more fun!

MAZES

Box Maze

Make a maze by setting up a trail of boxes and cartons of various sizes with both ends cut out. Plan several blind alleys to throw the players off as they crawl through. Play this game in teams or by yourself . . . perhaps even blindfolded! . . . and using a timer, see how quickly you can get to the end of the maze.

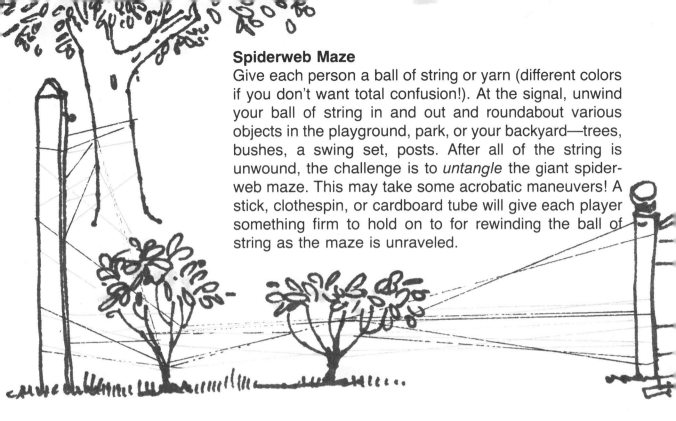

Spiderweb Maze

Give each person a ball of string or yarn (different colors if you don't want total confusion!). At the signal, unwind your ball of string in and out and roundabout various objects in the playground, park, or your backyard—trees, bushes, a swing set, posts. After all of the string is unwound, the challenge is to *untangle* the giant spiderweb maze. This may take some acrobatic maneuvers! A stick, clothespin, or cardboard tube will give each player something firm to hold on to for rewinding the ball of string as the maze is unraveled.

Have a Ball!

Hundreds of games can be played with just one piece of equipment . . . a *ball* (big or small, soft or hard, rubber or leather, Styrofoam or plastic . . . even a rolled-up sock will do in a pinch!). Whether you bounce it alone, play catch with a friend, or join a neighborhood softball game, a ball will provide hours of entertainment. Dodgeball, kickball, tetherball, volleyball, spud, and four-square are probably familiar games, but here are a few that may be new to you. Now go have a ball!

BALL ON THE WALL

There are dozens of ways to play this game—or make up your own rules. All you will need is a wall (or a slanting roof) and a ball with a good bounce. For "onesies" (as in Jacks), you can throw the ball against the wall, catching it on the fly just *once.* For twosies, you might let the ball bounce twice before you catch it. Threesies could be three claps before catching the ball on the fly. How would you continue the game to seven or eleven? You can play this game by yourself or compete against a friend to see who finishes first.

STOOP BALL

If you haven't enough space to play a regular game of baseball, try one that city kids have enjoyed for years. All you need is a front stoop and two teams of three or four players each. The first batter up throws a small, bouncy ball at the steps as hard as she can. She is *out* if the ball is caught on the fly by a player on the other team; she gets a hit if the ball is caught after one bounce, a double if the ball lands in the street and bounces twice before someone catches it, a triple when the ball bounces three times, and a home run if the ball goes all the way across the street without bouncing at all. *Be sure to look out for cars.* Keep track of the hits, runs, and innings, just like baseball.

KEEP IT IN ORBIT!

Form two circles, one inside the other, with the outside group standing and the inner players lying on their backs, heads toward the center. The object of the game is to keep a large ball (like a beach ball) going back and forth between the two circles without letting it touch the ground. The inner players *kick* the ball to the standing players, who bat it back with their hands, and so forth until someone misses. How long can you keep the ball in orbit?

BLANKETBALL

Divide into two teams, each with a tarp or blanket and a large ball. Holding on to the edges of the blanket with the ball in the center, the teams practice throwing the ball high into the air and catching it.

There are many ways to play blanketball. You could start playing the game by throwing *one* ball back and forth from blanket to blanket until one team misses. Next, one team could toss its ball up high and then quickly duck out of the way, letting the other team move in to catch it. Or, at a signal, each team throws its ball *at the same time* to the opposite blanket. You might also try having four players hold on to the corners of the blanket, toss up the ball, then quickly drop the blanket for four other players to grab *before* the ball can hit the ground.

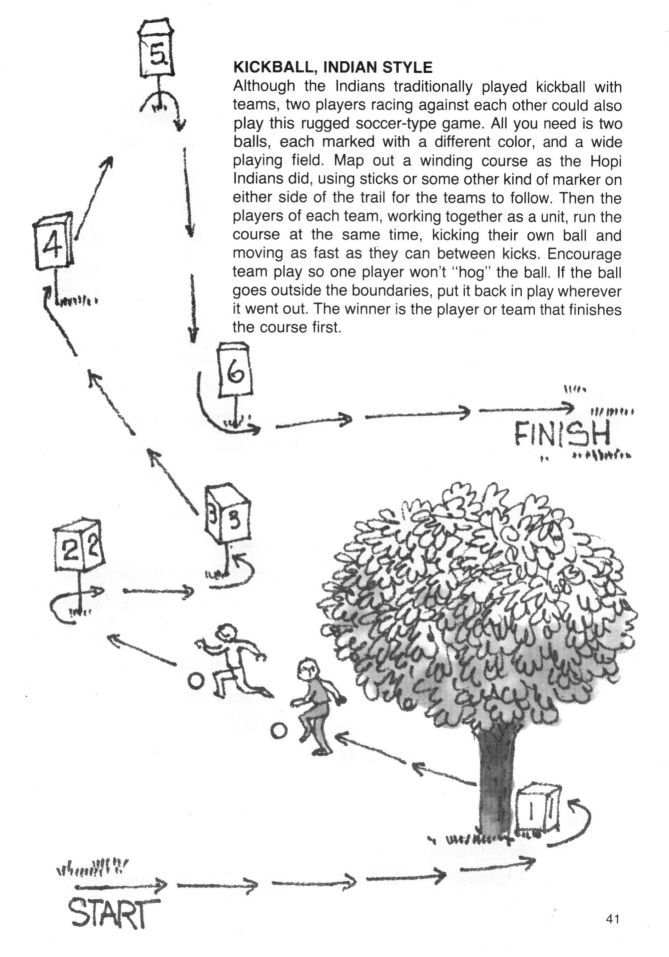

KICKBALL, INDIAN STYLE

Although the Indians traditionally played kickball with teams, two players racing against each other could also play this rugged soccer-type game. All you need is two balls, each marked with a different color, and a wide playing field. Map out a winding course as the Hopi Indians did, using sticks or some other kind of marker on either side of the trail for the teams to follow. Then the players of each team, working together as a unit, run the course at the same time, kicking their own ball and moving as fast as they can between kicks. Encourage team play so one player won't "hog" the ball. If the ball goes outside the boundaries, put it back in play wherever it went out. The winner is the player or team that finishes the course first.

FINISH

START

41

Miniature Golf

Dreaming up your own miniature golf course is a project that can take you as far as your imagination will go! Scrounged materials, brightly painted and designed around a theme, will challenge both the designers and the golfers.

There's no need to set up an entire golf course all at once. A few holes will give you plenty of practice. You can pick the materials up when you're finished and rearrange them another day.

First find a clear area in your backyard or playground, using any natural features like hills or mounds. You can also make these yourself out of papier mâché, piles of leaves or sand, and pie pans turned upside down.

Find an old doormat, heavy woven placemat, or carpet sample to mark each starting point or *tee-off* area.

Mark off the *fairway* boundaries with sticks or small stones. Then design a variety of obstacles such as ramps, alleyways, and tunnels for the ball to go through. Use materials like cardboard, box lids with holes cut in the sides, corrugated paper, long tubes or pipes, wood planks, and croquet wickets. To make the game harder when approaching the green, set up hazards like *sand traps* and *water holes* (shallow baking pans filled with sand or water). If a ball goes into one of these hazards, the player must pay a penalty by adding two points to her score.

For the *greens,* lay down large cardboard shapes or pizza trays with a three-inch hole cut in the center for the cup. An empty tin can on its side or a box with an arch cut in one end will also work. Number each green, perhaps with a cloth or paper flag attached to a stick.

Now borrow a putter and a golf ball, or use a long stick or broom and a small rubber ball, and PLAY GOLF! As you go through the course, count the number of times you hit the ball. Golf is one game where the player with the *lowest* score wins.

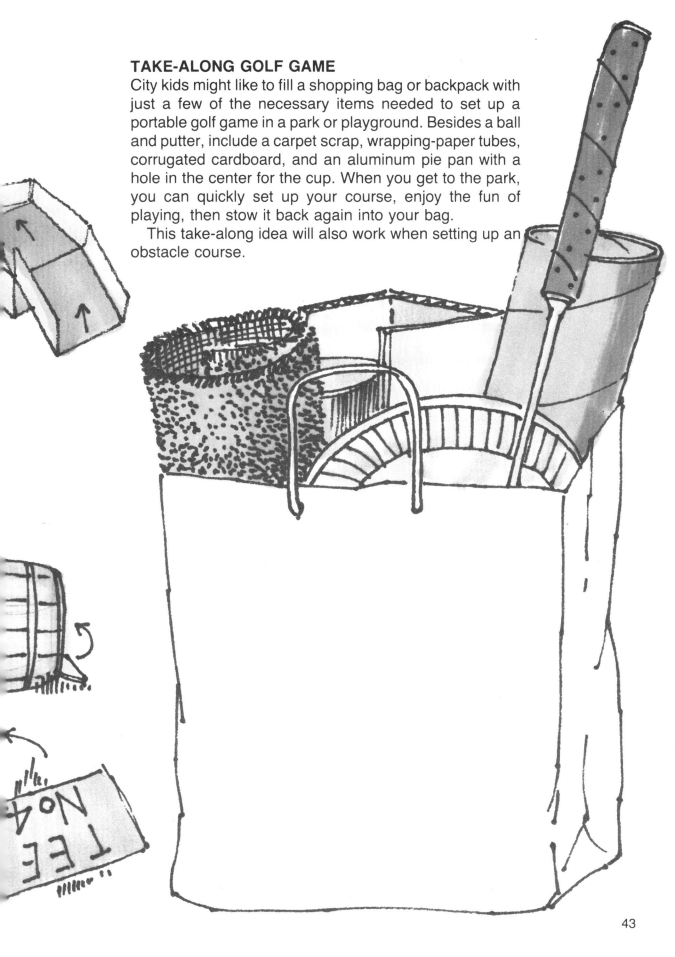

TAKE-ALONG GOLF GAME

City kids might like to fill a shopping bag or backpack with just a few of the necessary items needed to set up a portable golf game in a park or playground. Besides a ball and putter, include a carpet scrap, wrapping-paper tubes, corrugated cardboard, and an aluminum pie pan with a hole in the center for the cup. When you get to the park, you can quickly set up your course, enjoy the fun of playing, then stow it back again into your bag.

This take-along idea will also work when setting up an obstacle course.

TEE No4

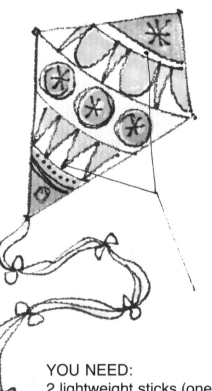

Kite Flying

Kite flying is a much older pastime than jumping rope. In 200 B.C., a Chinese general used a kite to measure the distance between his troops and an enemy fortress. He flew it low over the structure, then measured the length of the kite string that was used.

Did you know that the word *kite* comes from a bird of the same name in the hawk family? A flying paper kite resembles the kite bird's long, graceful glide. Kites can be made in almost any shape you can think of, with the diamond-shaped one the most traditional. You might enjoy experimenting with shapes like a hexagon, a box, a fish, or other animals. The sky's the limit! Here are instructions for a **DIAMOND-SHAPED KITE.**

YOU NEED:

2 lightweight sticks (one slightly smaller than the other) or pine lattice (flat pieces of wood available at a lumberyard)

lightweight paper, a grocery bag, or a large sheet of wrapping paper or newspaper

cloth scraps

scissors

pocketknife

glue

tape

heavy string or cord

paints or markers

a ball of kite string for flying

stapler

YOU DO:

1. Cut small slits in the ends of each stick.
2. Lay them crosswise and tie or lash them together in the middle with heavy cord.
3. Wind a long piece of string around the ends of the sticks through the slits and pull it taut, making a framework for your kite.
4. Lay the frame down on your paper; then trace and cut a cover, allowing 1 extra inch all around.
5. Before attaching the cover, paint or color a large, bold design that can be seen from the ground.
6. Fold the cover over the frame and attach it securely with glue or staples. Reinforce the edges with tape if you wish.
7. Make a tail by tying a few paper or cloth strips onto a long string.
8. Finally, attach a piece of string to your kite at two points for the bridle (as in illustration). Tie on the ball of string and you'll be ready to go fly your kite!

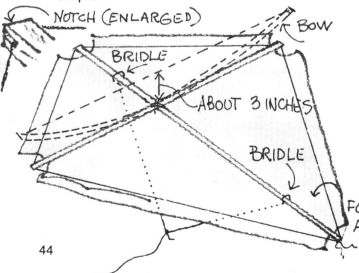

NOTCH (ENLARGED)

BOW

BRIDLE

ABOUT 3 INCHES

BRIDLE

FOLD OVER AND PASTE ALL AROUND

Tips for Successful Flying

1. A large, well-balanced kite is easiest to fly.
2. The tail (six times the kite's width is best) helps keep it upright.
3. Choose a day with a soft breeze; it shouldn't be too windy.
4. Find a large, open space with no trees or utility poles.
5. At least 100 feet of strong kite line is required.
6. Turn your back to the wind and let your line unwind quickly and smoothly. You don't need a running start.

CITY KITE

Here's a small, three-dimensional kite that's easy to put together and will fly high in the air over a city lot.

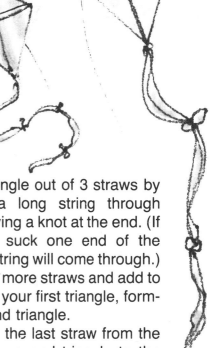

YOU NEED:
6 drinking straws
thin plastic wrap, typing or tissue paper
crepe paper
a ball of lightweight string
glue or tape

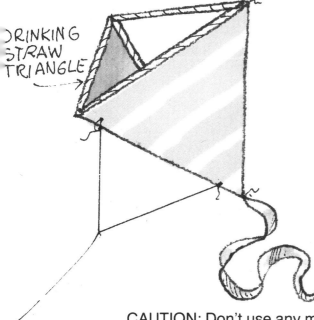

DRINKING STRAW TRIANGLE

YOU DO:

1. Make a triangle out of 3 straws by threading a long string through them and tying a knot at the end. (If you gently suck one end of the straw, the string will come through.)
2. Thread two more straws and add to one side of your first triangle, forming a second triangle.
3. Now attach the last straw from the top of your second triangle to the bottom of your first triangle with string or tape, and you will have a geometric shape called a *tetrahedron* (see illustration).
4. Measure and cut out plastic wrap or tissue paper to cover two sides of the kite. Then tape or glue it around the straws.
5. Attach a long (about 3 feet) tissue or crepe paper tail to the bottom of the kite. Tie on a string bridle and your ball of string, and away you go!

CAUTION: Don't use any metal on your kite or fly it in the rain. This can be very dangerous because the wet line or metal can *conduct static electricity* from the clouds right down to you.

FRISBEE

Frisbee, now an international pastime, got its name from the Frisbee Pie Company in Ohio where children began tossing around the empty tins. In the latest craze, "guts Frisbee," this flying saucer even made it to the Rosebowl for a world tournament, where it zoomed through the air at speeds of over 75 m.p.h.!

There are dozens of tricks and games you can play with a Frisbee or two, including relays, horseshoes, and feats of skill. Frisbee golf courses are springing up all over the country; some people even play this game from a wheelchair. Get a partner and add these ideas to your bag of Frisbee tricks:

1. Spin it, twirl it, and catch it on your finger.
2. "Hike" it between your legs or behind your back, then catch it the same way. Can you juggle several disks at one time or switch hands?
3. Play a four-square team game trying to keep the Frisbee moving in the air as long as possible. If it touches the ground, it goes over to the other team.
4. And finally, have two teams compete in "ultimate" Frisbee, combining *all* of the above games and techniques . . . anything goes!

If you're ever in Washington, D.C., look for the lowly Frisbee now on display at the National Air and Space Museum of the Smithsonian Institution.

Jump Rope

Jump ropes have been around for a long time; and many of the rhymes that go with jumping rope are the *same* ones your parents and grandparents enjoyed. Try some of these catchy jingles while you're jumping:

> *Rooms for Rent*
> *Rooms for rent, inquire within,*
> *When I move out, let (Mary) move in.* (Jumper moves out, new child named moves in.)

> *Millie, Mabel, and Sam*

Millie
Millie drank some marmalade, Millie drank some pop,
Millie drank some other things that made her stomach flop;
Whoops went the marmalade, Whoops went the pop,
Whoops went the other things that made her stomach flop.

Mabel
Mabel, Mabel, set the table and don't forget the sugar,
Mustard, vinegar . . . and the red, hot pepper! (This is the signal to turn the rope as fast as possible.)
How much pepper can you take?

Sam
Sam, Sam, the dirty man
Washed his face in a frying pan.
Combed his hair with the back of a chair
And danced with a toothache in the air.

Each generation of kids makes up its *own* rhymes. Why don't you?

BACKYARD CRAFT SHOP

What could be a better place to do all those messy craft projects than outdoors, where space and spills are never a problem! You can make all kinds of creations, from a giant papier mâché hamburger constructed right on the grass to a tiny pinecone porcupine that can be fashioned at your backyard work table or on your front stoop. Don't worry about dripping paint or glue—outdoor cleanup is a breeze!

Sculpture

PAPIER MÂCHÉ

The easiest and best-known way to make papier mâché is the strip method.

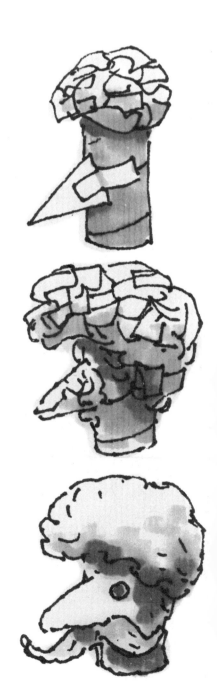

1. First decide on what object or free-form shape you want to make: an apple or an orange, a mask, a puppet head, an animal or figure, or whatever you dream up.
2. Use rolled or crunched-up newspapers, tubes, balloons, plastic containers, or bottles, and masking tape to form the basic shape.
3. Cut or tear newspapers into narrow strips and dip them into a mixture of white glue and water that is the consistency of thick pea soup. Slide each strip of paper through your thumb and forefinger to remove any excess liquid.
4. Wrap the strips around your shape, continuing until you have five or six layers.
5. Let your object dry overnight. Then sand the rough edges and decorate with tempera paint. When the paint is dry, shellac, for a shiny, long-lasting finish.

If you are making a large figure or structure, you will need to support it with a frame (called an *armature*) made of cardboard tubes or boxes, rolled newspapers, or coat hangers taped together. Or use scraps of lumber or chicken wire formed into a basic shape. For additional support, stuff crumpled newspapers into the nooks and

crannies of your framework. When you use chicken wire, weave paper strips in and out of the holes to form the first layer.

Hints

1. Use wide strips of newspaper to speed up the process when you make large objects.
2. Alternate layers of regular black and white newsprint and colored comic strip paper to help you spot any areas that you have missed.
3. Crisscross the newspaper strips to add strength.
4. For small items requiring no framework or to add features or accessories to larger objects, you might want to make a papier mâché *mulch.* Soak bits of newspaper for several days in a glue or paste mixture. After squeezing out the moisture, use the mulch as you would clay.
5. Apply paper toweling for your final layer to provide a smooth surface for painting.

FUN DOUGH AND SAWDUST CLAY

Flour or sawdust provide the basic ingredients for another kind of sculpture.

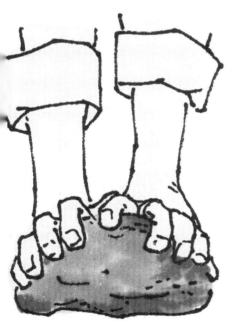

Fun dough is easily made by mixing 3 cups of flour with 1 cup of salt and 1 to 1½ cups of water, plus ¼ cup cooking oil to make it pliable. Pour the water in slowly, mixing until you get the right consistency (like cookie dough). Food coloring or a pinch of powdered paint can be added to the water. Knead well, roll into a ball, and store in an airtight jar or plastic bag in the refrigerator until you are ready to use it.

Sawdust clay will make good use of all that leftover sawdust from your carpentry projects. Mix together 2 cups of sawdust, 1 cup of flour, 1 teaspoon of salt, and 1 to 2 cups of water.

With the dough or clay, you can make plaques (use your fingers or a rolling pin to press ferns, leaves, weeds, flowers, pinecone petals, feathers, shells, and similar items into the clay); sculptures of people, animals, and other creatures; ashtrays, bowls, and so forth.

When making large sculptures, build the clay on a wire frame nailed or stapled onto a base. After the clay hardens, paint and then shellac it.

SOAP SCULPTURE

Soap is the perfect medium for simple sculpture. It's not expensive and can eventually be recycled in the bathtub! Soap looks something like marble, yet is soft enough to carve with an ordinary *table knife.* For best results, use brands that are soft and easy to carve, like Ivory, Dove, and Camay.

Choose a simple shape to sketch and then make an outline on the soap with a pointed stick. Brace your thumb against soap as you carve, cutting *slowly* and *carefully* · · · mistakes are hard to repair and so are fingers! Gradually cut away the large areas of excess soap from the background. To chip out a V-shaped piece, make a small cut just above the outline and a second cut that meets it at an angle. Continue turning the soap as you work.

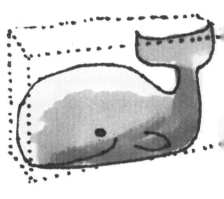

For the finishing touches, a potato peeler, paper clip, toothpick, orangewood, or popsicle stick are useful tools to make indentations and outlines and to give a textured look to the surface. If you want to add features or join two pieces of soap together (for example, a head and body), use a straight pin or a round toothpick. Fill in small holes or cracks with a paste made of soap shavings and water. Then smooth off your finished carving by dipping it in warm water for just a second and rub it with your fingers or with a damp watercolor brush. If you want to add decorative color to your sculpture, use your watercolors or a thin coat of tempera paint diluted with water.

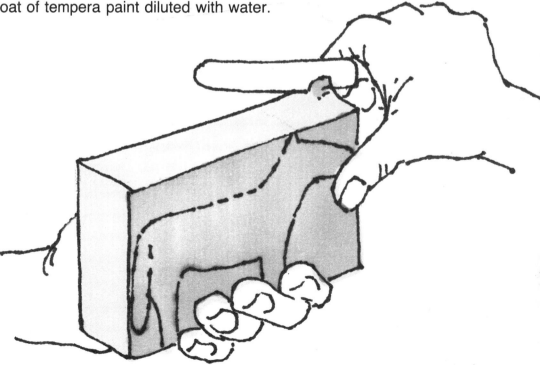

PLASTER SCULPTURE

You can carve a *plaster* "block" just like you did a bar of soap. Pour plaster of Paris mixed with water* into a cut-off milk carton, margarine tub, or a greased tin can. When the mixture is dry, remove from the container (just peel away the milk carton).

Use your soap-carving tools to sculpt decorative bookends or a paperweight. Leave the plaster as is or dab on paint with a sponge for a marbleized effect.

*The directions on the box will give you the correct proportions.

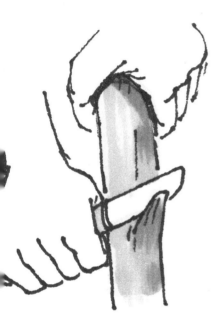

WOODEN WONDERS

Carving or whittling things out of wood is easy to do since the only tools required are a sharp pocketknife and sandpaper. Look for a stick or a piece of soft wood on the ground, or buy some at a hobby store—they're not expensive.

Before making anything, practice on a wood scrap, and remember, *always whittle away from you!* For your first carving project, draw a simple outline on a piece of wood and carve it out, stroke by stroke. Finish by sanding until smooth.

In the past, there were few store-bought toys, so people made their own, mostly from wood. Many of these "folk toys" use principles of physics and are baffling even today. The *buzz saw,* for example acts like a top, but spins on a string, making a singing noise like a buzzing saw. It is simply a large button or a disc attached to wooden handles by a long string. Whittle two handles and then insert the string through holes drilled in both the handles and in the disc. Pull the handles apart and watch the disc twirl around!

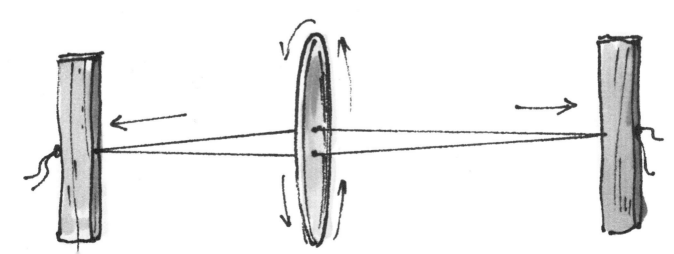

Whimmydiddle

You will need a hardwood stick about six to ten inches long and two to three inches wide for the body, a thinner stick for rubbing, a smaller twig for the rotor or propeller, and a nail about a half-inch to an inch long. Peel off the bark and sand any rough edges. Make six to ten notches evenly spaced along the top edge of the main stick. Drill a hole in the end of it for the nail. Then drive the nail through the twig and into the body so it can rotate. Now take the small stick and rub it briskly back and forth across the notches. As if by magic, the propeller will turn! These movements are called *gee* (right) and *haw* (left).

If your rotor doesn't turn and reverse easily, keep carving it down or deepen the notches.*

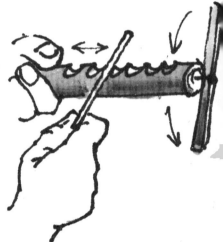

*The sticks should be cut from green trees like maple, oak, or witch hazel. Mountain laurel is the twig used in the southern highlands, where this is a traditional toy.

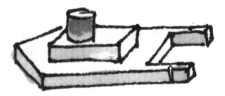

Paddle-Wheel Boat

You'll have hours of fun playing with this boat powered by a rubber band. First, carve a pointed hull from a rectangular piece of white pine or balsa wood. Then glue or nail a square block on top for the cabin and two dowels for the smokestacks. For the paddle wheel, cut slots in two pieces of wood as shown in the diagram. Glue the paddle-wheel pieces together and slip several rubber bands around them, fastening the loose ends to the two grooves in the end of your boat. Wind up the rubber-band motor (backward). Set your boat in the water and watch what happens.

Walking Stick

Many hikers enjoy using a walking stick. Select a sturdy tree branch, peel off the bark, and cut it to the right length, leaving yourself some growing room. If you can find one with a large knot at the top, it makes a nice grip. Carve decorations in your stick and then shellac or stain it.

Batik

Batik, the art of making designs on cloth with hot wax or paraffin, can be difficult, but here is an easy way to do it outdoors without using hot wax.

YOU NEED:

old pillowcase, hanky, cloth, T-shirt, scarf, and so forth
Jubilee Kitchen Wax
box of cold-water dye
water
large bowl or pan
stick
rubber gloves (optional)

YOU DO:

1. Draw your design on a clean piece of cloth, T-shirt, scarf, or whatever you want to decorate. If the fabric is new, wash, rinse, and dry it first.
2. To make a design, apply Jubilee Kitchen Wax to the fabric. You can squeeze the wax directly from the bottle, use a paint brush, or just your fingers. Let the wax dry.
3. Make a cold-water dye solution in a large bowl or pan, following the directions on the box. Dip the fabric into the dye, gently swishing it around with a stick or plastic spoon. Wherever there is wax, the dye cannot get through to color the cloth.
4. Remove the cloth, rinse it in cold water, and lay it out in the sun to dry. You could also dry it indoors using a clothes rack or dryer. Rub off any remaining wax, and your finished design will appear.

If you want to add more colors, it's best to rinse, dry, and reapply the wax before each dunking in the dye bath. Start with the lighter colors like yellow and then use the darker ones. When washing your fabric, be sure to use cold water since hot water may cause the dye to run.

Tie-Dyeing

Tie-dyeing is similar to batik, except that instead of using the wax to create the design, you tie off the parts that you don't want dye to reach. The fun is that no two pieces ever come out exactly alike! You can fold, twist, or crumple your fabric into bunches or even into a ball, and tie it tightly in several places with string, nylon, thread, or rubber bands. (Africans often tie their cloth around a stick.) Clips or clothespins can also be used for interesting effects. A piece of fabric folded into quarters will make a well-balanced design.

Here are two different ways of tie-dyeing cloth that are particularly suited for the out-of-doors. Tie in "found" objects, such as stones, acorns, shells, pinecones, peach and plum pits, bottle caps, marbles, beans, bolts, and screws. Or you can sandwich your cloth between two pieces of bark, twigs, or popsicle sticks and then tie it in several places to form a kind of splint.

YOU NEED:
cloth
box of dye
spoon
water
old pans
string
scissors
newspapers or clothesline

YOU DO:
1. Dip the tied fabric into the dye solution, following the directions on the package of dye. Use plastic, stainless steel, or enamel pans or bowls.
2. Remove the fabric from the dye solution, rinse it in cold water, and then wring it out.
3. Now comes the most exciting moment. *Carefully* cut off the strings and watch your original design unfold.
4. Spread the cloth out on newspapers or hang up on a clothesline to dry.

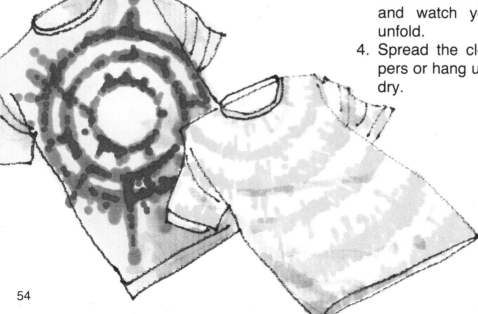

Experiment with several colors by drying the cloth and tying off new places between dippings. What happens when a yellow design is placed in a pot of blue dye? Red? Green?

Tips
1. Wear rubber gloves—unless you want to dye your fingers, too.
2. For best results, practice first on some rags.
3. Fabrics suitable for tie-dyeing are cotton, unbleached muslin, flannel, toweling, linen, and corduroy. Avoid synthetics like polyester blends or nylon because they don't take the dye as well.
4. Just as in the batik, don't use light colors over the dark ones because they won't show up as well.

Sand-Casting

This activity can be done in a sandbox, at your craft table, or best of all, at the beach.

YOU NEED:

shoebox, egg-carton lid, or other shallow container
stick
coffee can or other disposable container
plaster of Paris
water
pebbles, shells, twigs, beach glass, and other "found" objects.
paper clip or wire

YOU DO:

1. Fill your mold with moist sand—or just hollow out a place directly in the sand to make free-form blobs.
2. Make patterns in the sand with your hand or a stick, and then use pebbles, shells, twigs, beach glass,* and other items found in nature for texture.
3. Mix plaster of Paris and water in a large coffee can or other container. Stir with a stick until the mixture is the consistency of heavy cream. Then pour one or two inches of plaster into the mold. Insert a paper clip into the damp plaster for hanging.
4. Let the plaster harden for approximately a half-hour. Then gently lift your casting out of the box and brush off any excess sand.

Note: Plaster hardens quickly and can't be washed out, so use only utensils and containers that can be thrown away. Remember: always put plaster into a garbage can, *never* down the sink.

Beach glass, a plentiful "treasure," is unfortunately the result of careless litter. Constant contact with sand and rocks can change a jagged chip off a broken bottle into a frosted, smooth-edged collector's item! Bits of smooth beach glass can be used in mobiles and wind chimes, wall decorations, mosaics, driftwood sculptures. They are particularly beautiful when viewed with the light shining through.

Sandpainting

Sandpainting is an old art form handed down by the Navaho and Pueblo Indians. Try "painting" with sand just as the Indians do.

YOU NEED:
clean sand
tempera or powdered paints of various colors (or fabric dyes mixed with water)
jars and bowls with lids for mixing and storing
heavy cardboard or pieces of wood
white glue
brush
spray shellac

YOU DO:
1. Mix a little sand with some paint or dye (do one color at a time). Drain off the excess liquid, and spread on paper towels until thoroughly dry.
2. Spoon each color into a separate jar, paper cup, or empty salt or spice shaker.
3. Draw a picture on the wood or cardboard, and decide on a color for each section. (The Indians often put on a dark- or natural-colored sand background first and then layered on more sand, giving a three-dimensional look.)
4. Brush glue into one *small* area at a time, or make an outline and then sprinkle on the sand. Use your fingers, a spoon, or a paper cone if you don't have a shaker. After a few minutes, tap the picture and return the excess sand to its container.
5. Spray on shellac to seal your picture. Frame and hang.

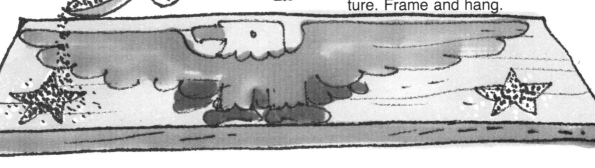

For added texture, glue on yarn, seashells, sticks, dried coffee grounds, bits of pinecones, crushed eggshells, melon seeds, or birdseed. You could also make "paint" by mixing cocoa, instant coffee, paprika, mustard, chili powder, or blue detergent with your sand.

OTHER SAND IDEAS

Ferns or leaves make interesting patterns. Brush glue on the veined side. Then press the leaf down on colored construction paper or cardboard, lift off quickly, and sprinkle on sand.

Glass or clear plastic containers can be made decorative by pouring in layers of colored sand. For a wavy effect, poke a stick into each layer, causing the colors to trickle down.

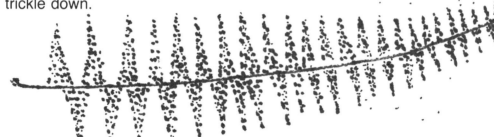

Preserving Flowers

DRIED FLOWERS

What could be a nicer wintertime gift than a bouquet of dried summer flowers? The best time to pick flowers for preserving is early in the morning but after the dew has disappeared. Select flowers in different stages, from bud to full bloom. Then cut the stems on a slant to the desired length, strip off most of the leaves, and tie the flowers into small bunches. Hang upside down in a warm place to dry away from direct sunlight and drafts for about two weeks.

Another way to preserve flowers is with *silica gel* (sodium silicate), which can be purchased from a florist, craft shop, or drugstore. The gel absorbs moisture quickly and preserves the natural colors of the flowers. Pour about 1½ inches of silica gel into a shallow, airtight container. Place each flower upside down in the gel, spacing them so they don't touch. Put the cover on for two or three days for small, delicate flowers and five to seven days for heavy ones. Don't overdry! You'll need to experiment and learn the correct timing by trial and error. P.S. A microwave oven will dry flowers in a jiffy!

Delicate	*Heavy*
baby's breath	dahlias
violets	black-eyed Susans
begonias	mums
alyssum	large marigolds

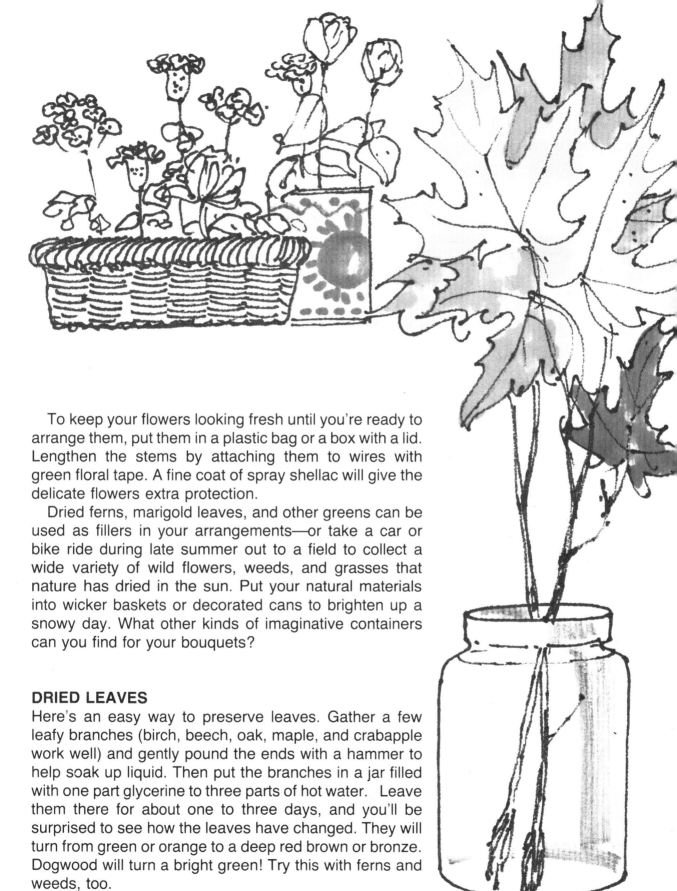

To keep your flowers looking fresh until you're ready to arrange them, put them in a plastic bag or a box with a lid. Lengthen the stems by attaching them to wires with green floral tape. A fine coat of spray shellac will give the delicate flowers extra protection.

Dried ferns, marigold leaves, and other greens can be used as fillers in your arrangements—or take a car or bike ride during late summer out to a field to collect a wide variety of wild flowers, weeds, and grasses that nature has dried in the sun. Put your natural materials into wicker baskets or decorated cans to brighten up a snowy day. What other kinds of imaginative containers can you find for your bouquets?

DRIED LEAVES

Here's an easy way to preserve leaves. Gather a few leafy branches (birch, beech, oak, maple, and crabapple work well) and gently pound the ends with a hammer to help soak up liquid. Then put the branches in a jar filled with one part glycerine to three parts of hot water. Leave them there for about one to three days, and you'll be surprised to see how the leaves have changed. They will turn from green or orange to a deep red brown or bronze. Dogwood will turn a bright green! Try this with ferns and weeds, too.

Nifty Nature Crafts

CORNCOBBERY

The earliest settlers in America made toys for their children out of corncobs and cornhusks. You can make some too. The next time you eat fresh corn, just save the cobs. Scrape off any kernels, rinse the cobs in cool water, and hang them up to dry for seven to ten days. When they feel prickly, they are ready to be made into dolls and animals. Use the cob for the body and add round toothpicks or lollipop or popsicle sticks for arms, legs, ears, and other features. If you want to cut the cobs into rounds or other shapes, soak them overnight and slice immediately (while still soft) with a serrated knife. To color your cobs, add dye to the soak water or paint them later. Dry some corn silk in the sun for hair, mane, tails, etc.

Indians made the first cornhusk dolls in America, and they gave them to the Pilgrims as gifts. Here is a simple way to create one:

1. For the arms, roll a cornhusk tightly around a pipecleaner or wire. Tie the husks with string at each end to form hands.
2. For the head, roll ¼-inch strips of husk into a ball or use them to cover a small piece of cotton, a bead, or a Styrofoam ball.
3. Wrap *long* strips over the head, insert the armpiece, and tie above to form the neck and below to make the waist.
4. Split the husks below the waist to make legs for a boy doll, or trim the bottom edges for a skirt.

Dress your doll by attaching additional husks of various lengths to the body to make trousers, skirts, and other clothing. Wrap large, square pieces of husk around the arms for puffy or straight sleeves. Aprons, caps, scarves, or shawls made of scrap materials and ribbons will add the finishing touches. Draw the face with felt markers or glue on small beads, buttons, or seeds for eyes.

Cornhusk balls were used by country children for throwing and kicking. To make one, dip several husks into a bowl of warm water. Roll one husk into a ball. Then wrap several other husks around it and tie securely with string. Let the ball dry for two or three days. Repeat these steps over and over until the ball is the size you want. To make the toy more colorful, you can wrap it with yarn.

APPLEHEAD DOLL

1. Peel an apple and remove the core.
2. Sprinkle salt inside the hole and then stuff it with cotton.
3. Now carve away a little bit from each side of the apple to form a face.
4. Using the tip of a potato peeler, scoop out eyes, a nose, and a mouth and put a dried bean inside each hole.
5. Then push a short stick or pencil through the middle of the apple and poke it into an egg carton turned upside down or a can of sand.
6. To preserve the head, brush on lemon juice and salt well.
7. Leave your applehead in a warm place for two or three weeks until it is completely dry.
8. Add a clear varnish for a finished look, and pin on yarn hair if you wish.

CREEPY CREATURES

To make a creepy creature, use pinecones, large shells, rocks, or horse chestnuts for the body. Glue on seeds, twigs, pieces of bark, and small shells for arms, legs, and facial features. Mount your finished creature on a Styrofoam, cork, or driftwood base.

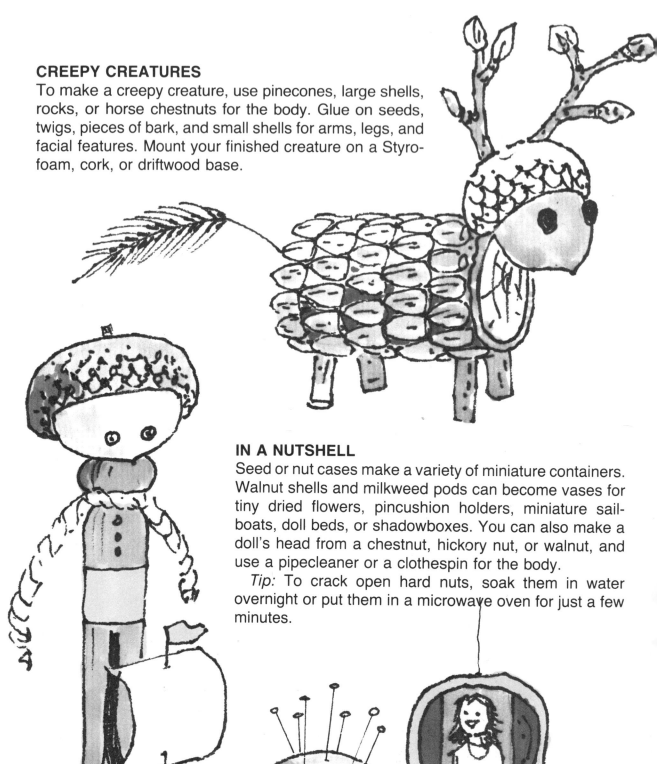

IN A NUTSHELL

Seed or nut cases make a variety of miniature containers. Walnut shells and milkweed pods can become vases for tiny dried flowers, pincushion holders, miniature sailboats, doll beds, or shadowboxes. You can also make a doll's head from a chestnut, hickory nut, or walnut, and use a pipecleaner or a clothespin for the body.

Tip: To crack open hard nuts, soak them in water overnight or put them in a microwave oven for just a few minutes.

EXPLORING NATURE

Take a Walk

Have you ever *really* taken a good look at what's around you? Learning to be an observer is a real art and takes practice. How high would you score on an LQ ("Looking Quotient") test? Think of a familiar route—one you've probably taken dozens of times, perhaps to school or to a friend's. Jot down on a piece of paper what you remember seeing before. Then with your list in hand, retrace your path, looking *carefully* and using your eyes like a telescopic lens or magnifying glass. You may be surprised at the many new and interesting things you've never noticed before: a striped awning, a fire hydrant, storefront signs, shadows on the sidewalk, a cat stretching in the sun, a flower growing out of a crack, graffiti on a wall. Keep track of your discoveries. Can you double or triple your original list?

It might be fun to send several people on the same route. Compare lists and see what different things each person has observed.

OTHER IDEAS

Draw a rough map of your route. Then using your list as a reminder, mark in the points of interest and familiar landmarks. Add the points of the compass. (North is usually at the top of the map.)

Make crayon rubbings by placing a piece of shelf or typing paper over something textured: bricks, manhole covers, house numbers, tree bark, and so forth. Take along a sketch pad or your pinhole camera (see p. 65) to keep a record of your walk.

1. BIG TREE ON CORNER.
2. IRON FENCE.
3. FOUR STREET LIGHTS.
4. HARDWARE STORE, BOOK STORE, GROCER, CLOTHING STORE.
5. HOUSE, HAUNTED
6. RIVER UNDER BRIDGE.
7. STONE WALL
8. LIBRARY
9. SUN FLOWERS

Nature Sketching

Outdoor sketching is a fascinating hobby for the city or the country that can take just an hour or two or even an entire afternoon. First assemble your equipment—a sketch pad or clipboard and paper, a soft drawing pencil, charcoal, crayons, colored chalk, or paints—and then stow all of it in a backpack or a bag.

Look around for something that interests you: a budding tree, a clump of weeds or wild flowers, a cloud formation, an iron fence, a wooden gate, windowpanes, and so forth. Once you've found a likely spot, seat yourself comfortably and get to work.

Notice the details of the scene before beginning to draw or paint—like the pattern in a brick wall or the distinct design formed by the branches, leaves, and the tapering trunk of a tree. To help you isolate or frame a particular area or object, look through a "naturalist's camera," made by cutting an opening one-inch square in a small piece of cardboard. Watch for repetitions of lines and shapes. Where do you see light and dark patches or subtle changes in color? Sketching can help you discover things in nature by making you more observant of clues that lead to their identity.

Some artists like to begin with a few quick "thumbnail" sketches for practice before tackling a large picture. When you are ready to start your picture, draw in the outlines with charcoal or a pencil and then fill in the areas of color with paints, crayons, or chalk. The details can be done last in a darker shade with a pen or a small watercolor brush.

Whatever art materials you choose, do some experimenting first. Watercolors are tricky because they dry quickly, so plan ahead. Acrylic paints also dry quickly and are easy to use since you can paint over your mistakes. Pastel drawings should be sprayed with shellac or hairspray so the chalk won't smear.

It's fun to return to the same place at different times of day to record how things look in the *changing* light. You might also want to choose one of your favorite sketches to do again in a more finished way at home. (Here's where your thumbnail sketches and color notes will come in handy.) Save your favorite paintings and drawings to exhibit at a neighborhood art fair or to use as gifts for your family and friends.

Photography

The word *photo* in Greek means "light," and that's what photography is all about. To become aware of the effects of sunlight on objects all around you, squint or look through a cardboard tube. Notice where the light stops and shade begins. What do you think causes shadows? Find out by going on a *shadow hunt.* Look for an interesting shape and "capture" the shadow by slipping some paper under it and tracing the outline. See if your friends can guess what the real object was.

Taking pictures with a store-bought camera is fun, but using one you have made yourself is even more fun and a little like magic, too. Photography can be a simple or complicated hobby; it's up to you how involved you want to become. There are all kinds of books you can read and experts to consult, including people at your local camera store who will be glad to give you tips.

PINHOLE CAMERA

You can make a simple pinhole camera, which is basically a box with a tiny hole in it that works just like your eye.

YOU NEED:
box with a tight lid (shoebox or round
    oatmeal or grits container)
black paint or construction paper
heavy-duty aluminum foil
masking tape
cardboard
glue
scissors
pin
photographic paper (8 x 10 is
    standard)

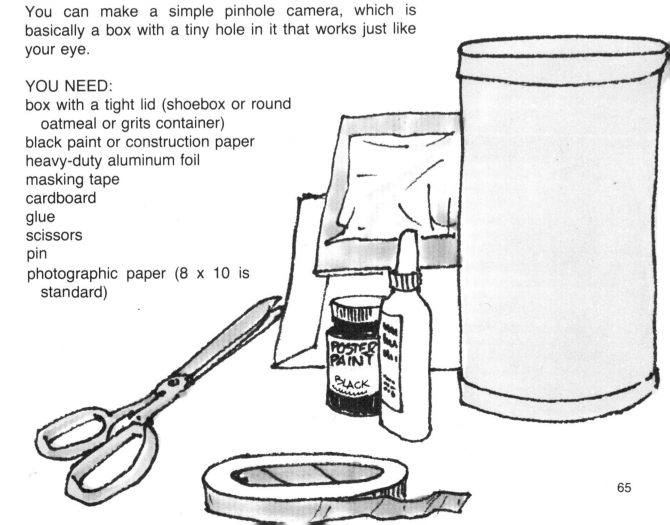

YOU DO:

1. Paint or spray the inside of your box, or glue down black construction paper in it.
2. Cut a small hole (about one inch square) in the center of the lid.
3. Cut a piece of foil slightly larger than your square and make a frame (the same size as the foil) with two pieces of cardboard, gluing the foil in between.
4. Tape the cardboard frame securely over the opening in the lid and poke a tiny hole in the center of the foil with the pin (turning it to make smooth edges).
5. Tape a cardboard flap over the hole for a "shutter."
6. Now place a ring of masking tape, sticky side out, in the bottom of the box directly under the pinhole. This will later hold the photographic paper in place.

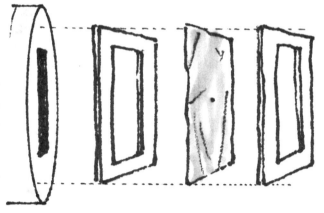

(If you would prefer to make a pinhole camera that uses an Instamatic film cartridge rather than photographic paper, consult the Boy Scout photography manual.)

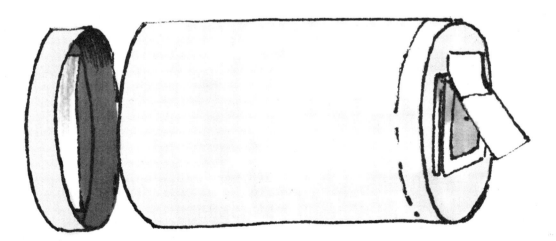

Now that your pinhole camera is completed, you are ready to think about a subject for your picture. Use your cardboard "naturalist camera" to plan an artistic composition just as you did before sketching.

Taking the Picture

1. Go into your clubhouse "darkroom" or a closet, and under a "safe light" (a flashlight covered with yellow cellophane or a yellow light bulb), carefully open a package of photographic paper. A bright light will ruin the film by overexposing it.

2. Cut the paper to size (4 x 5 inches is average) and secure it, shiny side up, onto the tape inside your camera. Replace the lid.

3. Then go outdoors and, with your back to the sun, point the camera (pinhole in front) toward an object. Lift the flap for about 1½ minutes on a bright, sunny day (3 minutes if it's cloudy). When taking a *portrait,* it's best to steady the camera on something, like a tree stump, box, or stepladder, since it takes 2 to 3 minutes to expose the film.

   Do you think *you* could sit still for that long without wiggling? How about your pet gerbil?

4. After taking each picture, remove the paper from the camera under a safe light. Slip the photo paper inside an envelope and seal it before taking it to the camera store to be developed into a print.

Nighttime Experiment

If you would like to understand how a pinhole camera works, here is a quick way to find out. Remove the top and bottom of a round cereal container. On one end, glue aluminum foil; on the other, waxed paper. Punch a pinhole in the center of the foil. Then, holding the foil side close to a bare light bulb, move the box back and forth (focusing) until an image appears on the waxed paper. How does the image look? What would happen if the hole were larger? Answer: The image would become blurred from too much light entering the box.

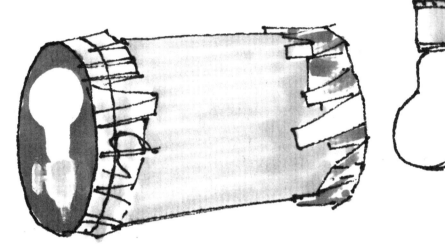

SUN PICTURES

Did you know that you can take outdoor pictures without *any* camera at all? First collect some small, natural objects, such as leaves, ferns, weeds, or flowers, or a few flat household items like a cooking utensil, string, wire, or paper clips. Then inside, away from direct light, place a sheet of blueprint paper (available at a camera or hobby store), blue side up, on a piece of cardboard (or inside a box) and arrange the objects on it in an interesting design. (To hold them in place, tape them down or put a piece of glass or heavy clear plastic on top.) Now carry your covered box outdoors and expose your design to the sun for a few minutes. Hurry back inside, remove the objects, and look at what you and the sun created!

If you want your sunprints to be permanent, you will have to fix them by dipping each one into a solution of ¼ cup of 3% hydrogen peroxide dissolved in 2 cups of water. Rinse the print in cool water, blot between paper towels, and hang up to dry. Soon your picture will be ready to frame.

Backyard Zoo

Did you know that three-quarters of all known living creatures in the world are insects? There are 750,000 kinds at least, and no doubt a large number of these are ants, many probably living between the cracks of your sidewalk or in your own backyard. Studying ants is an intriguing pastime, since they are "social insects"; they live and work together by the thousands in a complex network of underground chambers and passages.

Ants are identified by what they do: a queen who lays the eggs; males whose only job is to mate; workers; undeveloped females who feed and tend the larvae (hatched eggs) and repair the nest; and soldiers who guard the queen, fend off enemies, and even capture "prisoners" to add to the labor force.

ANT FARM

To view this busy society at work, build an ant farm. Here is an easy kind to make that will let you watch the ants for a day or two. Dig up a few ants and put them in a small glass jar. Place it upside down inside a larger one: then fill the large jar and the space between with moist sand. Poke tiny holes in the lid and cover the jar.

← you may use cheese cloth

To make a more permanent ant farm with a picture window, you will need two pieces of glass (8 x 10s from old picture frames work well) and four strips of wood ½ inch thick and 1 inch wide, cut to fit the glass. Glue the strips of wood to the edges of the glass, leaving a 1-inch opening at the top of the frame. White silicone bathtub caulking can be used instead of glue for a better seal. When dry, reinforce all of the edges with 1½-inch cloth tape. (See illustration.)

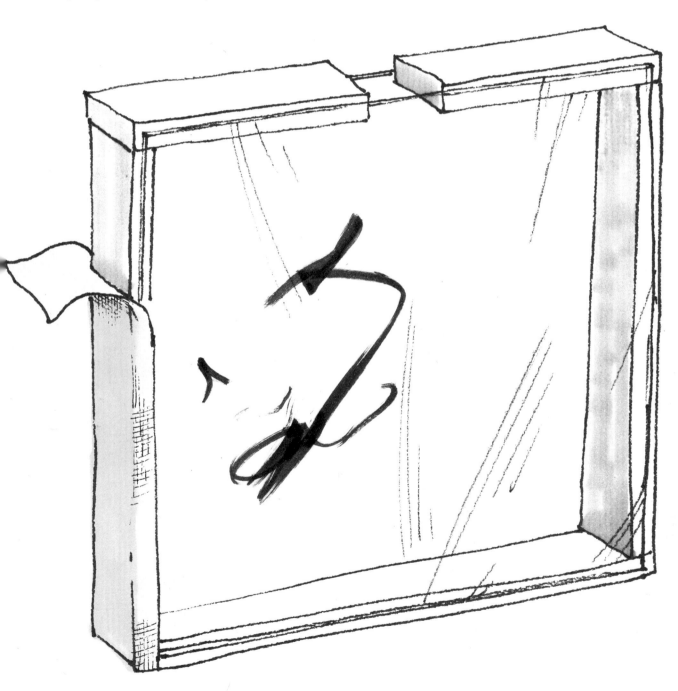

To begin your new colony, look for ants under rocks, in the grass, near curbs, and between the cracks in cement. You can usually attract them with a little sugar water in a jar placed on its side. When digging for ants, try to find a queen, since she is essential to the growth of your colony. Being much larger than all of the others, she will be easy to spot.

Quickly funnel the ants and dirt into the opening in the frame and then add *more* dirt to the halfway mark. Place a piece of sponge on top of the soil under the opening. Use an eyedropper to water the sponge about once a week to keep the soil moist but not wet. Drop in tiny bits of food every few days—bread, nuts, apples, bananas, honey, or molasses—but *do not overfeed! Caution:* Unless you want to be invaded by an army of ants, keep the hole plugged with a piece of cotton!

Because ants prefer to work in the dark, keep the farm covered for a day or two. You'll be amazed at the progress of these energetic little builders when you lift the cover and discover a series of new rooms and interconnecting tunnels. Can you find these special compartments: the busy nursery, the pantry for food storage, or the ants' garbage dump? This same type of glass house can also be used for studying burrowing earthworms.

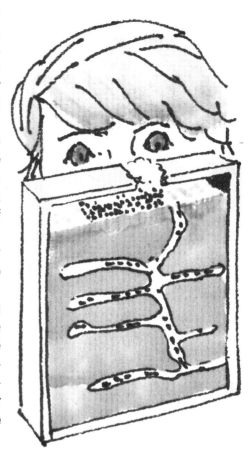

INSECT AND ANIMAL CAGES

You might want to house some other insects like *crickets* or *beetles* in your backyard or back-porch zoo. A simple cage can be made from popsicle sticks or tongue depressors, glass jars, or tin cans covered with screening. After you have studied their habits for a while, let them go.

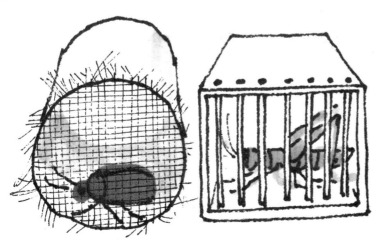

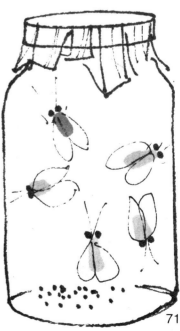

Butterflies

Butterflies are not only beautiful to look at; they are helpful insects since they control pests and pollinate flowers. Did you know that though a butterfly gathers food with its tongue, its sense of taste is actually in its feet?

If you can find a caterpillar, try to "hatch" it into a butterfly and watch one of nature's miracles! Put the caterpillar into a large jar. Cover the jar with a lid with holes or with gauze or cheesecloth held on by a rubber band. Add leaves from the plant or tree where you found it since each caterpillar feeds on only one kind of plant. Give your caterpillar a fresh leaf every few days, and soon it will spin a cocoon. In a few weeks a butterfly will emerge. Leave it alone for twenty-four hours, until it is dry and the wings are strong, and then set it free.

Spiders

Another animal certain to be hiding in a "cozy corner" or in your backyard habitat is the eight-legged spider. (You may be surprised to find out it is not an insect at all since it doesn't have the required three body sections and six legs.) To make a temporary home for this unusual pet, place two twigs and a drop of water in a glass jar along with the spider. Feed your spider some live flies or mosquitos, and it may spin a web to catch them, right before your eyes! These delicate-looking silk threads are strong enough to trap caterpillars and locusts—insects much larger than the trapper. Although scientists believe that there are fifty thousand different kinds of spiders, only the brown recluse and the black widow can be harmful . . . and even these, like all other spiders, are shy.

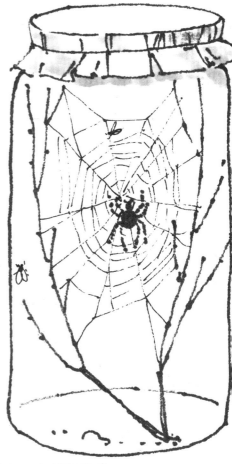

Should you discover an unoccupied web, you will have the makings of a beautiful picture! Spread newspapers around the grass and bushes under the web, and then gently spray paint it from both sides. Carefully slip a piece of construction paper against one side and cut the web away from the branch or whatever is holding it. Let the web dry before mounting it between glass to preserve the spider's intricate workmanship.

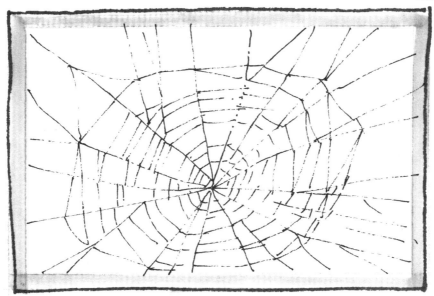

Indoor Pets

Indoor pets will live happily out-of-doors when the weather is warm. Your backyard zoo is an excellent spot for rabbits, hamsters, guinea pigs, and gerbils. Bring their cages outside and find a protected place for them. If you have new animals, all that is needed to make a cage for them is a wine or fruit crate; chicken wire or screening for the top and bottom; nails; and some scrap lumber for legs (to keep the cage off the ground—at least six inches for air to circulate and debris to fall through). Make a top that can be removed for feeding and for taking your pets out to play.

Set the cage in a shady spot and always have plenty of food and fresh water on hand. All of these animals eat pellets as their main staple. You can buy these in bulk at a pet store or supermarket. Lettuce, carrots, celery, and bits of fruit are a special treat but should never replace the pellets that are needed for good digestion and nutrition.

WATER FEEDER

Here is a nifty way to keep your pets' water supply clean and fresh.

1. Just poke two holes about two to three inches from the open end of a large juice can.
2. Fill the can with water; then place a large tinfoil pie pan or saucer over the top and, using both hands, carefully turn both containers upside down.
3. Now every time your pet takes a drink, a little water will trickle into the saucer and the rest will stay in the can, free from leaves, bugs, and debris.

Although guinea pigs, hamsters, and gerbils should be brought inside when the temperature dips below 40°F, rabbits can live year round outdoors in a hutch like this, as long as it has an extra closed compartment for warmth.

74

Birds

What is it about birds that makes them so fascinating? Is it because *they* can fly and we can't? Nature has adapted birds perfectly for flying, with incredibly large, powerful muscles and a long wingspread. Their bodies are streamlined because of interlocking feathers, and lightweight because of balloonlike air sacs and hollow bones.

CANARD GLIDER

How about building a glider or a kite shaped like a bird to get some firsthand knowledge of flying? A glider flies on its own power and looks like a bird in flight. This glider is named after the canard (French word for *duck*), which flies in a straight line and lands slowly. It is designed with an "elevator" in front to give it its lift.

To make one you will need a piece of paper 8½ x 11 inches for the wing and one 5 x 5 inches for the elevator.

For the elevator:

1. Cut diagonally across your 5 x 5 piece of paper.
2. Fold it in half, measure ⅜ inch along the folded edge, and mark with a straight line.
3. Then fold the elevator wings down along this line to form the keel.

Now for the wings:

1. First fold the large piece of paper in half lengthwise, unfold, and fold back the two upper corners to the midline.
2. Now fold toward the center. Then fold the wings together, allowing 1⅛ inches along the center fold for the keel or backbone.
3. Bend each wing down along the keel line and clip 1¼ inches off the nose.

To assemble the glider, put a paper clip on the nose of the elevator. Then slip the elevator into the keel slot of the wing, and tape it as shown. Now try flying your glider!

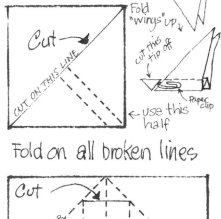

Fold in half

Fold "wings" up

cut this tip off

use this half

Cut

CUT ON THIS LINE

Paper clip

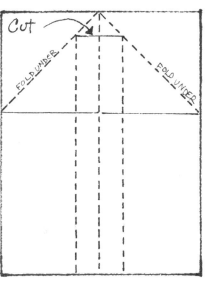

Fold on all broken lines

Cut

FOLD UNDER

FOLD UNDER

Tape this end, too

Tape this end

Paper clip inside

BUILDING A SIMPLE BIRDHOUSE

Invite the birds to raise their young in your backyard by offering them room and board.

Did you know that different birds like different types of homes? When designing your birdhouse, you should have a particular occupant in mind, one that you have seen in your neighborhood. For the house, you'll need to consider the color, placement, exposure to sun and wind, overall dimensions, size of opening, and so forth. Consult a book or bird expert or write to the U.S. Department of Agriculture for a detailed list of specifications.

Here are some general hints. Except for purple martins, which love the social life of apartments, all birds like privacy and therefore prefer to live in single-family dwellings, placed far apart. To make a bird family really feel welcome, make your house of wood (metal is too hot) and paint it with light earth tones (even though bright colors appeal to you). Set the entrance away from the wind and up high off the floor of the house to protect the young. Drill holes at the top for ventilation and at the bottom for drainage. The roof should be sloping with an overhang so the rain can run off.

NESTING

Most birds have both a winter and a summer home and an amazing instinct to return to the same place to nest every spring. The nest-building instinct is even more incredible! Each new generation of parents uses *exactly the same* design, materials, and location that all of their ancestors did. For example, robins use mud, and hummingbirds use spider webs to hold their "nurseries" together. Did you know that the females are the chief builders in the bird kingdom? Give the birds a hand at nest building by scattering bits of cloth, straw, string, cotton, yarn, and paper on the ground in the early spring.

The only time to go *nest collecting* is in the fall or early winter when the bird families have departed, and nests can be easily spotted in the bare branches. Don't feel you are stealing, since birds never use the same nest twice. Spray on a coat of shellac to preserve your finds. Display them in a glass or plastic box, or mount them on a forked branch in a clay base. Then you can carefully study the construction methods of these ingenious nest builders.

FEEDING

During warm weather, birds find their own insects, worms, seeds, and grain but appreciate gifts of fresh fruit and water. In the winter, however, birds *depend on you for nourishment.* If you decide to start feeding birds, be consistent about keeping it up. Birds will come back faithfully when they are certain food is always there. Check the supplies daily, or your new friends could starve.

You can make a homemade *bird feeder* by cutting a window in a plastic bleach or milk bottle. Or use a hollowed-out gourd, coconut, orange, or grapefruit half to hold the seeds, or spread suet or peanut butter on a pine-cone. Mesh bags, plastic berry baskets, and logs with holes cut at intervals also make ideal suet holders. Bird feeders can be hung from a tree or bush or placed on a windowsill. Let the birds share in your holiday celebration by putting out extra strings of cranberries, popcorn, dried fruit, or peanuts.

Recipes for the Birds

Mush

Mix 2 cups yellow cornmeal, 2 cups sugar, 2 cups ground suet, 1 cup flour, and 2 cups water. Cook and stir 5 minutes. Keep in refrigerator and put some out each day.

Bird Pudding

Mix raisins, bread crumbs, cooked potatoes, and oatmeal together. Pour bacon grease over the mixture and let harden in a plastic cup, fluted muffin wrapper, or empty tuna can.

There are lots of scraps from your kitchen that also will give the birds a feast: cake, bread, and cracker crumbs; cereal left in the bottom of the box; popcorn kernels; and so forth. You might even want to hang a stale doughnut on a tree branch. It's helpful to know that birds that are insect eaters, such as blue jays, will eat suet in the winter, while sparrows and cardinals eat only seeds, and robins prefer fruit and berries.

Did you know that you can tell what and how a bird eats just by the *shape of its feet and bill?* For example, sparrows hop on sturdy feet and have strong, short beaks for crushing seeds; herons have long legs, necks, and bills for wading and fishing. How has nature equipped hawks, pelicans, and ducks for catching their food?

BIRDWATCHING

Once you've attracted the neighborhood birds, you can get a close-up view of them. Birdwatching is fun year round but is especially interesting in the spring season when birds are courting, mating, nesting, and feeding their young. Only "early birds" will catch a glimpse of their feathered neighbors at feeding time since it's usually between 4:00 and 7:00 A.M.! You can probably spot two or three kinds in your own backyard, but a bird walk in a nearby forest preserve or field will introduce you to even more species. (There are eight hundred different kinds in North America alone!)

Tips for a Bird Walk: Dress in dull-colored clothes and wear sturdy walking shoes (waterproof, if possible, for the early morning dew). Pick a clear day and always keep the rising sun at your back so you can observe the birds in their full color. Here is a checklist of what to bring along:

- ☐ bird guidebook
- ☐ notebook or pad
- ☐ pen or pencil
- ☐ binoculars (optional)
- ☐ camera (optional)
- ☐ picnic breakfast

To avoid frightening the birds, keep the group small— no more than five or six. Move slowly and quietly, talk in whispers, and when you sight a bird, "point and freeze." Because birds are curious creatures, you can attract their attention with a squeaky sound made by sucking against the back of your hand or with a bird whistle.

Identifying Birds

Once you know what to look for on your bird walk, you can play detective. First notice the overall size, shape, and color of unfamiliar birds. Important clues to solving the mystery of their names are field marks, spots, patches, stripes, and other markings on the tail, wings, breast, crown, or eye.

A trained observer can learn to spot the silhouette of a bird in the sky and will come to know its flight pattern—dipping, gliding, soaring, skimming—another tip-off to the bird's true identity. Will the real yellow-bellied sapsucker please stand up?

If you have a really good ear, you can learn to recognize *bird calls,* perhaps the best clue of all! Male birds sing to claim their territories, frighten off rivals, and attract females. If you have a tape recorder, you might want to take it on your bird walk to help you remember and imitate the songs of the birds in your neighborhood.

Backyard Garden

Designing, planting, and tending your own flower and vegetable garden will surely be one of the most satisfying projects of the summer! Begin early (in March or April or even earlier if your winters are mild) to look through seed catalogs and gardening books for ideas. Draw a diagram showing what seeds will be planted in each row, keeping in mind the height and spread of the plants when full grown.

Use this chart to help you choose some seeds that are easiest to grow in your garden.

FLOWERS	VEGETABLES	*HERBS
*marigolds	*carrots	parsley
zinnias	lettuce	mint
*sweet alyssum	beans	chives
bachelor buttons	*radishes	sage
hollyhocks	cucumbers	thyme
*petunias	beets	rosemary
periwinkle	spinach	basil
sunflowers	squash	
(grow giant ones	*bell peppers	
and roast the seeds	corn	
for eating!)	pumpkins	
	gourds	
	corn	
	popcorn	
	*peanuts	
	*tomatoes (really a fruit,	
	and one that needs a headstart indoors)	

Bachelor buttons and hollyhocks, chives, and mint are perennials that will come up automatically each year, just like dandelions. The rest of the flowers on this list are called *annuals* and must be replanted every spring.

* These grow well in a windowbox or flowerpot garden. See page 84

If you're adventuresome, you might want to plant some blue potatoes, giant elephant garlic, yellow radishes, peppers that look like bananas, or popcorn seeds that come in rainbow colors. These unusual varieties may be hard to find at your local gardening store, but you can probably get them by mail. You can send away for seed catalogs from these and other companies:

Burpee Seed Co., 3538 Burpee Bldg., Warminster, PA 18974

Gurney's, Yankton, SD 57078

Nichols Garden Nursery, 1190 N. Pacific Highway, Albany, OR 97321

George W. Park Seed Company, Greenwood, SC 29647

Stokes Seeds, Box 548, Buffalo, NY 14250

Thompson & Morgan, P.O. Box 100, Farmingdale, NJ 07727

When weather conditions are right, ask your parents where you can stake out a sunny spot in your yard (a 6 x 10 foot plot is ample), or use a nearby vacant lot, with the owner's permission. Dig up the soil with a spade or shovel and rake well to break up lumps and remove debris. For best results, mix in some fertilizer or home-made compost. To make compost, find a spot to pile up leaves, vegetable peelings, fruit rinds, coffee grounds, and so forth. Cover the pile with a dark plastic leaf bag held down by bricks. Start your pile in the fall and it will be ready for spring planting. (Peat moss or sand may be added if necessary for better drainage since they make the soil more porous.)

For a vegetable garden, mark off rows and place a stick at each end with a string tied between. Using the strings as guidelines, dig long, shallow troughs and sprinkle in your seeds *according to the directions* on each package. As a reminder, place each empty packet on top of the appropriate stick. (If you plant climbers such as beans or sugar snap peas, place them next to a fence or a trellis at the north end of your garden so they won't block the sun from the other plants.)

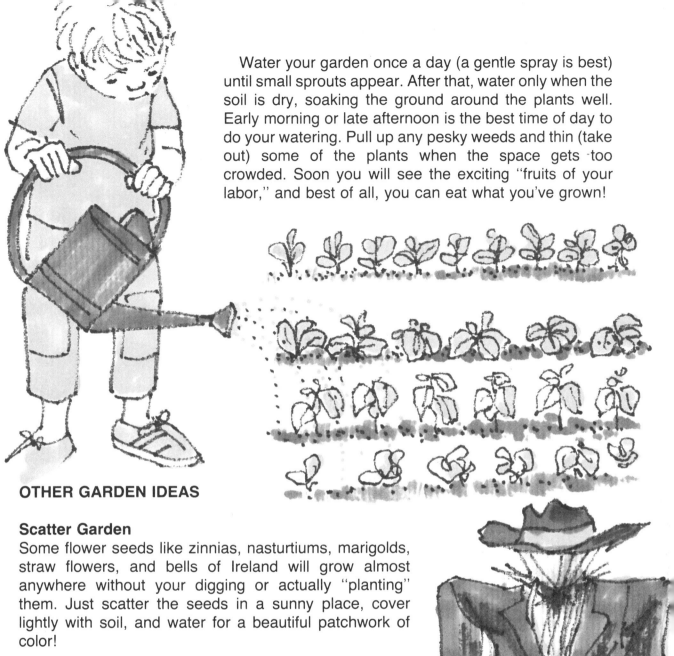

Water your garden once a day (a gentle spray is best) until small sprouts appear. After that, water only when the soil is dry, soaking the ground around the plants well. Early morning or late afternoon is the best time of day to do your watering. Pull up any pesky weeds and thin (take out) some of the plants when the space gets too crowded. Soon you will see the exciting "fruits of your labor," and best of all, you can eat what you've grown!

OTHER GARDEN IDEAS

Scatter Garden

Some flower seeds like zinnias, nasturtiums, marigolds, straw flowers, and bells of Ireland will grow almost anywhere without your digging or actually "planting" them. Just scatter the seeds in a sunny place, cover lightly with soil, and water for a beautiful patchwork of color!

Discourage Bugs, Crows, and Rabbits

You will have many garden helpers, including birds who are natural bug catchers. Attract them by making a birdbath from a shallow dish or plastic garbage can lid set off the ground. Change the water every day to keep it fresh. You can also rig up a scarecrow complete with broom, old hat, and some worn-out clothes stuffed with straw. Sprinkle a few mothballs or plant some basil near your lettuce and spinach to keep the rabbits from nibbling the leaves; marigolds will keep away tiny worms and aphids that dislike the smell and the bright orange color.

CITY GARDENS

If there is no available spot for a full-sized garden, don't give up. A *windowbox* or *flowerpot* garden will serve just as well. Find some wood scraps to make a sturdy box. Poke holes in the bottom for drainage, fill the containers with potting soil, plant some seeds, and you'll soon have a "patch of green." Herbs such as thyme, basil, and rosemary are also easy to grow and will spark up your meals later in the summer. (A few sprigs of basil growing on a windowsill will keep flies away!)

Geraniums, sunflowers, and even corn and tomatoes grow nicely in large clay pots, gallon cans, or plastic buckets. For drainage, punch holes in the bottom, put in a layer of small rocks, and then add potting soil, fertilizer, and a layer of peat moss on top. Check your small pots every day and be sure to water when the soil is dry.

Happy gardening!

What a Dandy Lion!

Do you know where the dandelion gets its name? Take a close look at a dandelion leaf. What does it remind you of? The French thought it looked like the teeth of a lion and named it "dent de lion."

Young dandelion leaves make a tasty spring salad. They have twenty-five times more vitamin A than tomato juice and fifty times more than asparagus! Gather the leaves when they are still reddish and curled before the bud has appeared; rinse well, and chill before serving with your favorite salad dressing.

Dandelion leaves also make a delicious tea. Older leaves that are large and dark in color are the best for brewing. Wash them thoroughly, and place them in a brown paper bag to dry in the sun for a few days. Crumble the "tea leaves" and place in a jar of water (1 teaspoon per cup), letting it "steep" in the hot sun for an hour or so. Add a little honey and you will have a delicious cup of dandelion "sun tea." For a refreshing drink with a wintergreen flavor, boil a few pieces of bark from a birch tree and add it to your tea. Have you ever tasted rose petal or pine needle tea?

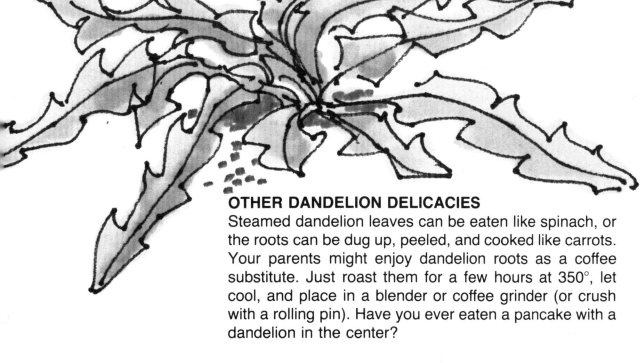

OTHER DANDELION DELICACIES

Steamed dandelion leaves can be eaten like spinach, or the roots can be dug up, peeled, and cooked like carrots. Your parents might enjoy dandelion roots as a coffee substitute. Just roast them for a few hours at 350°, let cool, and place in a blender or coffee grinder (or crush with a rolling pin). Have you ever eaten a pancake with a dandelion in the center?

CAMPING OUT

There is nothing more fun than hiking or backpacking through the woods and then sleeping out under the stars. How about setting up a campsite in your own backyard? Here you and your friends can pretend you are miles away from civilization, experiencing the same adventures and practicing similar routines and skills as backpackers and campers do in the *real* wilderness. City children will need to find a country cousin to visit for a camp-out!

Remember that the key to success is to *plan ahead.* First decide on the length of time you'll be in the "wilds" (eighteen to twenty-four hours is probably enough for the first try). Then make a list of necessary jobs, equipment, and acitvities. Divide the various chores among your group so everyone can share the responsibilities as well as the fun. Here is a sample to give you some ideas for making up your own list:

JOBS
menu planning
shopping
packing up
setting up campsite
wood gathering and
    fire building
cooking
cleanup
repacking equipment

EQUIPMENT
first-aid kit
extra clothing
backpack
sleeping bag
    or bedroll
ground cloth
tents or tarps
*Styrofoam ice chest
cooking and eating
    utensils
jackknife
flashlight
sports equipment

ACTIVITIES
hikes
games
crafts
photography
journal keeping
campfire songs
    and stories
stargazing

*Important for keeping food from spoiling.

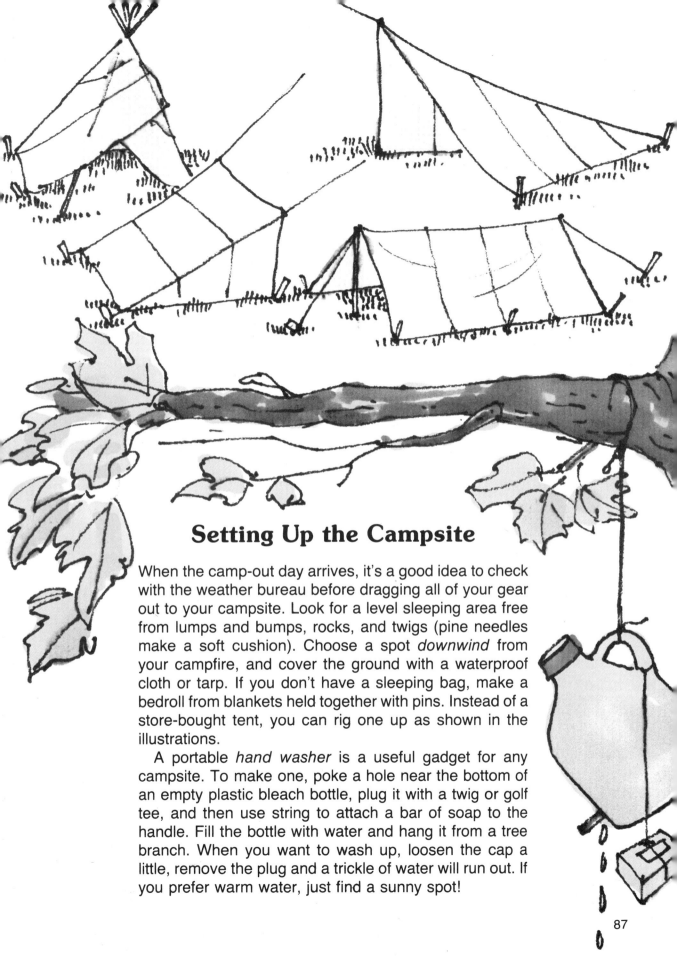

Setting Up the Campsite

When the camp-out day arrives, it's a good idea to check with the weather bureau before dragging all of your gear out to your campsite. Look for a level sleeping area free from lumps and bumps, rocks, and twigs (pine needles make a soft cushion). Choose a spot *downwind* from your campfire, and cover the ground with a waterproof cloth or tarp. If you don't have a sleeping bag, make a bedroll from blankets held together with pins. Instead of a store-bought tent, you can rig one up as shown in the illustrations.

A portable *hand washer* is a useful gadget for any campsite. To make one, poke a hole near the bottom of an empty plastic bleach bottle, plug it with a twig or golf tee, and then use string to attach a bar of soap to the handle. Fill the bottle with water and hang it from a tree branch. When you want to wash up, loosen the cap a little, remove the plug and a trickle of water will run out. If you prefer warm water, just find a sunny spot!

Hiking

Now that your campsite is all set up, how about a walk before dinner? Hiking in a nearby park or forest preserve or right in your own neighborhood is a great way to collect natural materials like feathers, pinecones, and leaves for craft projects.

BLAZE A TRAIL

Divide into two groups, the hares and the hounds, and play a hunting game. Give the hares a head start to mark their trail using stones or forked sticks as pointers.* See how long it takes the hounds to find where the hares are hiding. You could also play "Hansel and Gretel" and leave a trail of breadcrumbs and popcorn—the birds will enjoy feasting on the leftovers.

STRAIGHT AHEAD

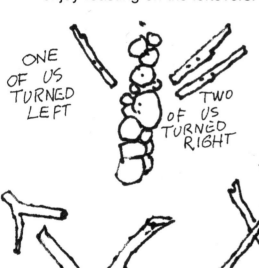

ONE OF US TURNED LEFT

TWO OF US TURNED RIGHT

WE ARE IN THIS CORNER OF FIELD

TURN RIGHT

FORK IN TRAIL — GO TO LEFT

THIS WAY TO CAMP

TURN LEFT

WE WERE HERE AT FOUR O'CLOCK

If you've walked far enough, you're probably ready to get back to your campsite and cook your own feast!

*Another way to leave trail clues is to use peeled sticks or tie bunches of weeds or grass onto low branches.

Cooking Out

FIRES

Everyone will agree that the best part of camping out is the food! Even the simplest fare tastes better when cooked outdoors over an open fire. Before deciding which cooking method to use, ask your parents for permission and find out about your local fire laws, always keeping in mind that fires can be dangerous. Here are some ideas for different kinds of fires and homemade stoves. Of course, you could always use your portable Bar-B-Q, but that's not roughing it!

First gather your firewood and sort it into three piles according to size: (1) tinder (crumpled paper, pine needles, and grasses), (2) twigs and sticks, and (3) logs.

Safety First

1. Have a bucket of water on hand before striking the first match.
2. Weatherproof wooden matches by dipping the tips into wax or nail polish. Store them in a plastic bag or a small tin Band-Aid or throat lozenge box.
3. *Never leave a fire unattended.* Cover with sand and dirt when you are finished. Be sure that it is completely out, and see that no live coals remain. If possible, pour water on the fire.
4. In case of a burn, cold water or ice applied *immediately* is best. Burn ointment is a good thing to have in your first-aid kit. Don't use butter or grease.
5. Use your fire to practice distress signals in case you ever need help in the real wilderness. Make a signal fire by adding wet leaves or small branches to your campfire to create puffs of smoke. The universal call for help is three rapid, steady signals. (These can also be made by flashes of light or blasts on a whistle.)

A Surefire Method

To start a fire without a match, you'll need two flashlight batteries stacked one on top of the other (old ones are okay) and a half-inch strip of fine-grade steel wool. Stretch the steel wool to a length of five or six inches. Holding one end of it against the bottom of the lower battery, rub the other end of the steel wool across the top battery. In a second a spark will appear! When it does, place it next to the tinder and blow on it to start the fire.

On a scorching hot day you can cook without any fire at all. Just let the sun's rays do the work! Have you ever tried to fry an egg on the sidewalk? A solar cooker works on the same principle. Try making your own solar oven or hot dog cooker using cardboard, aluminum foil, and wire as shown.

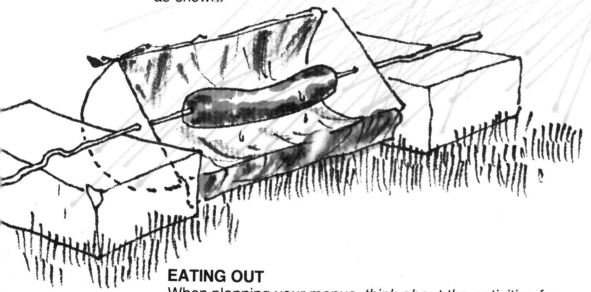

EATING OUT

When planning your menus, *think about the activities for the day.* There are many nutritious foods that can be quickly prepared for outdoor meals and snacks. Remember to keep all perishable foods, especially dairy products, meats, and mayonnaise, in a cooler or ice chest.

Breakfast should be hearty and easy to fix.

Swiss Birchermüsli

This is a nourishing backpacker's breakfast. Start with a granola or farola mixture (wheat germ, nuts, seeds, and honey) and add some pieces of cut-up fruit (apples, bananas, berries). Pour in milk (powdered milk mixed with water is fine) and top with yogurt.

Doughboys

Mix Bisquick and water until sticky. Fold around a green stick and toast over the fire until the dough is lightly browned. Pull out the stick and fill the center of the doughboy with margarine or butter and honey or jelly. Yum!

"Pancakes" à la English Muffin or Orange Cup

Cut an English muffin in half, dip into pancake mix, and fry in butter or margarine; or cut an orange in half, scoop out the pulp for your first course, then fill the "cup" with pancake or biscuit mix. Wrap in foil, leaving a little air space at the top, and bake in the coals for fifteen minutes.

Take-Along Cocoa Mix

YOU NEED:
3 cups confectioners' sugar
1 cup nondairy creamer
1 cup cocoa or carob powder
3 cups nonfat dry milk crystals
2 cups miniature marshmallows
(6 cups boiling water to be added later)

YOU DO:
Combine all of the dry ingredients in a mixing bowl and store in an airtight container. Add the water when ready to drink. This recipe will make 8 cups. For a single serving, place ¼ cup of the mixture in a cup and add 6 ounces boiling water. Stir until well blended.

For lunch you'll want just a sandwich or a light snack, especially if you are hiking. Then it's best to eat often, nibbling on small treats such as peanuts, toasted seeds, or trail mix (a combination of raisins and other dried fruits, nuts, sunflower seeds, and shredded coconut). These and other "pocket foods" like Walking Salad, a chocolate or carob bar, or M&Ms will keep your hunger down and your energy up!

Walking Salad

Cut off the top of an apple, remove the core, and scoop out some apple pulp. Chop it up with raisins, nuts, cheese, etc., stuff back into the apple, and replace the top. Keep in a plastic bag.

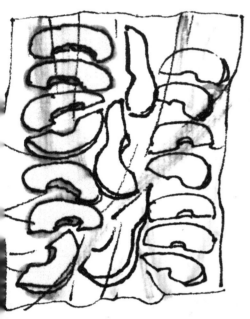

Fruit Leather

Cut fresh peeled fruit (apples, pears, peaches, nectarines) into pieces and dry them out in the sun on a rack (covered with plastic wrap) for 4 to 6 hours. *Or* bake overnight in your oven at 200° with the door left slightly open.

Peanut Butter Sandwich Spread

This spread is packed with protein. It can be made in advance and stored in a plastic container until you are ready to make the sandwiches. Mix together 1 cup of peanut butter or cream cheese with ½ cup of honey, ½ cup of crumbled crisp bacon (or commercial bacon bits), ½ cup of wheat germ, and 1 cup of drained, crushed pineapple or mashed banana.

Skillet Suppers

Save the big meal for evening when you have time to prepare and enjoy it. Hearty one-step dinners like *campfire soup* and *stew* can be cooked in a pot . . . or in a pouch made of heavy-duty foil. Combine chicken or hamburger, beef or lamb cubes with vegetables such as potatoes, onions, parsley, carrots, green beans, and/or tomatoes and a little water. Seal tightly and let simmer for about an hour.

Frypan Franks
YOU NEED:
1 tablespoon butter or margarine
1 cup water
6 frankfurters, sliced
1 small can peas and carrots
package dehydrated potatoes
⅓ cup milk
1 chopped onion
grated cheese

YOU DO:
Melt the margarine, add potatoes, water, and milk, and boil, stirring occasionally. Cook for 10 minutes and add remaining ingredients. Top just before serving with grated cheese. (Ham can be substituted for the hot dogs, and tomatoes for the peas and carrots.)

Frypan Bread goes nicely with your supper.

YOU NEED:
2 cups flour
1 teaspoon salt
3 teaspoons baking powder
6 tablespoons margarine or butter

YOU DO:
Sift together the dry ingredients and then cut the margarine or butter into small pieces. Mix well with a fork until grainy. You can make this bread dough ahead of time and store it in a plastic bag in the refrigerator until ready to use. (Will keep up to six weeks.) Stir in ⅓ cup of water and a cup of berries. Knead and shape into a cake about one inch thick. Fry in a heated, greased pan over the coals (or low heat) until nicely browned on both sides. Let the bread cool before eating.

Your entire dinner can be eaten out of just *one* cup: a wide-mouthed stainless steel, twelve-ounce container (known as a Sierra cup). You could also use a less expensive tin measuring cup or a heavy plastic one. Just wash it out and reuse for each course.

Top off your meal with a delicious dessert of toasted s'mores, pudding cones, or banana boats. For these last treats, pull a section of banana peel back and scoop out a piece to form a "dugout canoe." Fill the hollow space with chocolate or carob chips and marshmallow bits, replace the banana slice, wrap in foil, and bake in the fire for just a few minutes.

This unusual treat will keep for many hours without spoiling.

Pudding Cones

YOU NEED:
½ cup nonfat dry milk
1 package (4½ oz.) chocolate-fudge-flavor instant pudding (or any one of your choice)
1 envelope (1½ oz.) whipped topping mix
1¼ cup cold water
flat-bottom cones

YOU DO:
Beat until stiff (about two minutes). Then spoon into ice-cream cones. Wrap each one in plastic, if you make them ahead of time. Store in a muffin tin.

AFTER-DINNER CAMPFIRE

After dinner, relax around the campfire . . . join in the singing and storytelling, corn popping, and marshmallow roasting. How about some ghost stories or stargazing just before "taps"? Can you find the sailors' "nighttime compass," the North Star?

Word and theater games are especially fun around the campfire. Charades, Snap, and Add-a-Noise can be found in the game section (p. 36). Look for other ideas in the outdoor theater section (p. 107).

Late Night Snacks

No fair going inside to raid the refrigerator—get your midnight snacks ready before you put out the fire.

P.S. Since you'll wake up with the birds anyhow, why not take this chance to catch the sunrise with your camera or go on an early morning bird walk?

Neighborhood projects require plenty of cooperative spirit, ingenuity, and hard work and are well worth the effort! These special events are a great way to get all of the older and younger children, and even the parents and grandparents, together. Several of the projects that follow are possible money makers; others will perk up the dog days of August with lively entertainment; still others, like the country fair, will give you a chance to show off the results of your summer efforts from your backyard craftshop or garden.

Hold your get-togethers in someone's yard, garage, or alley; or get permission to block off the street or to use a parking lot, empty lot, or school playground.

Whichever event you tackle, get everyone into the act! Appoint committees for decorations, entertainment, printing and publicity, refreshments and the rest, and don't forget the treasurer and the cleanup crew. Although not everyone can be a "chief," no one's talents and interests will go to waste.

Fund Raisers

Do you need some new ideas for raising money? A bike shop, a backyard flea market, an arts and crafts fair, or even a "new-fashioned" lemonade stand featuring tasty health foods might be just the answer. Perhaps your group would like to support a worthy cause (such as your local library, animal shelter, or hospital), or you may just want to buy some equipment for a neighborhood project.

HEALTH FOOD BAR

Can you imagine summer without a lemonade stand? Give yours a new twist by featuring tasty health foods like carob, wheatgerm, or yogurt, instead of the usual soft drinks, candy, and ice cream. This novel refreshment stand will offer nutritious food and drink for any of your neighborhood events. All you will need is a bucket or Styrofoam chest filled with ice and a mixer, a blender, or a strong stirring arm—and someone to help with your expenses until the profits roll in and you can pay back the loan.

With these tempting recipes you'll be sure to attract many customers.

Drinks for the Stand

Easy Fruit Punch

Mix together several flavors of frozen or canned fruit juice, lemonade mix, and water. Add sugar-free ginger ale or lemon-lime soda and stir well. Serve in paper cups with an ice cube and perhaps a fresh strawberry floating on top.

Strawberry Shake-up

Pour ½ cup of milk, ¼ cup of strawberries (fresh or frozen), 1 tablespoon of wheat germ, and 1 teaspoon of honey into a bowl or a jar with a top; whip with an egg beater or shake until frothy.

Paper-Cup Popsicles

Whip up a batch of homemade popsicles to keep in paper cups in your freezer until needed. For every 2 cups of fruit juice or yogurt juice (yogurt mixed with frozen juice concentrate), add one or more of the following: ½ cup applesauce, 1 cup mashed bananas, 1 tablespoon grated orange or lemon rind, 1 cup crushed berries, 1 cup peeled, chopped peaches, 1 can crushed pineapple.

Watermelon Slush

Cut up chunks of melon (2 cups), remove the seeds, and put into a blender. Then fold the slush into ½ cup of whipped cream, chill in the freezer or an ice chest, and serve in paper cups with spoons.

Zesty Vegetable Juice

Mix chopped fresh vegetables such as carrots, celery, tomatoes, and cucumbers in a blender with some water or pineapple juice. Allow ½ cup of vegetables to each ¼ cup of liquid.

Carob Drink

In the blender, mix ¾ cup milk, 2 teaspoons of honey, ¼ cup of cocoa or carob drink powder, and ice cubes. Yogurt can be substituted for the milk, if you wish.

Food for the Stand

Snack-a-Bobs

Put chunks of meat and cheese, fruit, and fresh vegetables onto toothpicks. Salami, bologna, carrots, cucumbers, olives, grapes, strawberries, pineapple, and melon balls are a few examples of delicious "finger foods."

POW Bars

Mix ½ cup of honey or molasses, ½ cup of peanut butter, 1 heaping tablespoon of carob powder or cocoa, and 1 cup of powdered milk together and knead into a stiff dough. Then add chocolate chips, raisins, dried apricots, or shredded coconut. Shape into balls, logs, or long snakes and roll in powdered sugar or sesame seeds.

Bag-a-Snacks

Walking Salad, trail mix, (described in the camping out section) and other snack foods can be packaged and sold in cups or plastic bags.

You might also offer a bowl of apples, oranges, nectarines, peaches, grapes, bananas, and even some dandelion salad!

BIKE SHOP

If there are a lot of bike riders in your neighborhood, they probably could use some help with bike repairs. Why not open a bike shop in a corner of your yard or garage? Some of the services you could offer might be washing, waxing, oiling or greasing, pumping air, patching tires, or tightening loose parts. Have a tub of water on hand to check for leaky tires. If you charge for your services, your bike shop can become a summer money maker, as well as an interesting learning experience. And an added dividend is that your own bicycle will be in tip-top shape!

You might want to go into business for yourself and buy some new parts like bells and reflectors to resell to your customers. Check around to find the lowest price possible, either from a wholesale catalog or discount store, and to increase your profits, buy in quantity, if you think you'll have lots of customers.

To learn about maintenance and repairs, read a bike owner's manual or books on cycling and ask questions at a neighborhood bicycle shop.

"Bicycle Rules of the Road" (usually available free at libraries, schools, police departments, or wherever bicycles are sold) will give you handy pointers on safety and local traffic laws. You could incorporate these guidelines into a bicycle safety check as a special feature of your new shop. Here is a sample checklist:

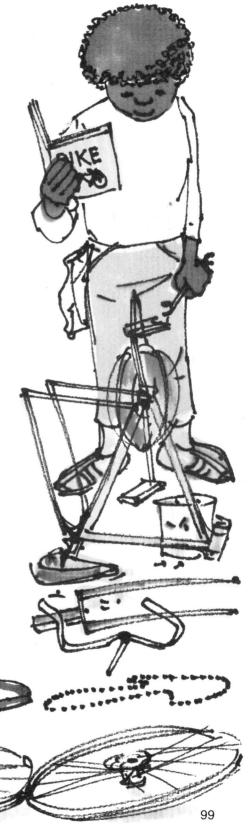

- ☐ brakes
- ☐ bell or horn
- ☐ lights
- ☐ bolts
- ☐ reflectors
- ☐ tires
- ☐ gears
- ☐ chain

Once you have mastered all the ins and outs of cycling safety, you can offer a course similar to driver's ed and then test your "students" on the rules of the road, awarding a "license" for a passing grade. Advertise your services early in the summer so that everyone's bicycle (and tricycle) will be all set for the Fourth of July parade.

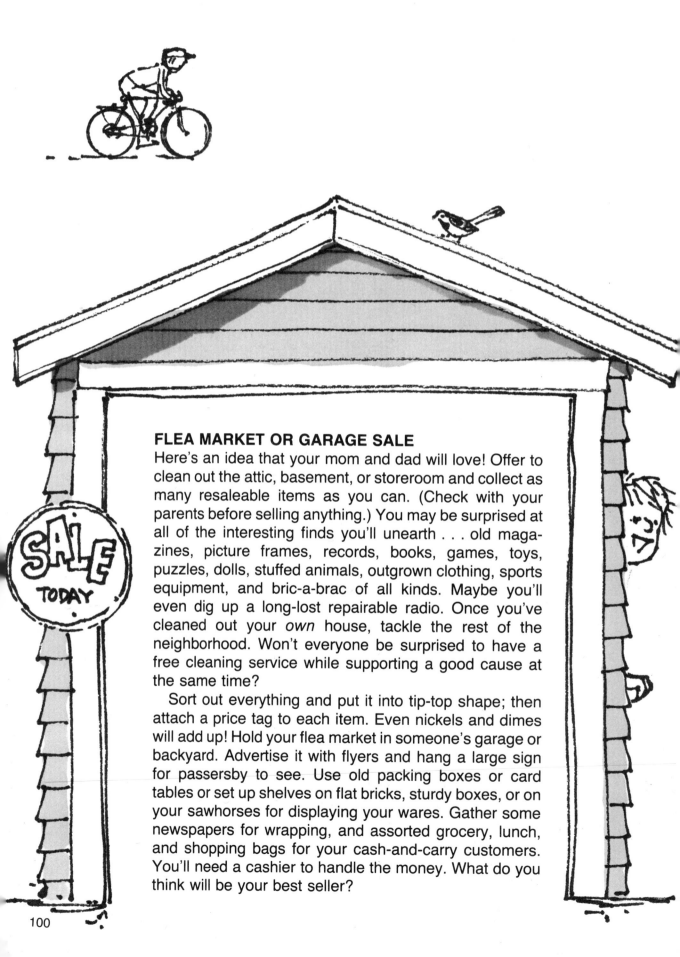

FLEA MARKET OR GARAGE SALE

Here's an idea that your mom and dad will love! Offer to clean out the attic, basement, or storeroom and collect as many resaleable items as you can. (Check with your parents before selling anything.) You may be surprised at all of the interesting finds you'll unearth . . . old magazines, picture frames, records, books, games, toys, puzzles, dolls, stuffed animals, outgrown clothing, sports equipment, and bric-a-brac of all kinds. Maybe you'll even dig up a long-lost repairable radio. Once you've cleaned out your *own* house, tackle the rest of the neighborhood. Won't everyone be surprised to have a free cleaning service while supporting a good cause at the same time?

Sort out everything and put it into tip-top shape; then attach a price tag to each item. Even nickels and dimes will add up! Hold your flea market in someone's garage or backyard. Advertise it with flyers and hang a large sign for passersby to see. Use old packing boxes or card tables or set up shelves on flat bricks, sturdy boxes, or on your sawhorses for displaying your wares. Gather some newspapers for wrapping, and assorted grocery, lunch, and shopping bags for your cash-and-carry customers. You'll need a cashier to handle the money. What do you think will be your best seller?

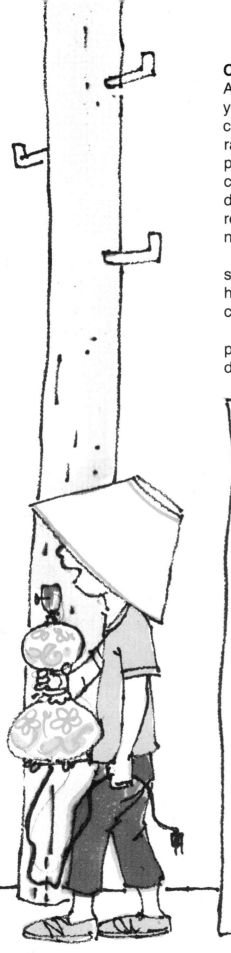

OUTDOOR SERVICES, INC.

Another good way to make some money and spruce up your neighborhood at the same time is to form work crews to pick up trash (cans, papers, and other debris), rake, sweep, and hose off front steps and sidewalks; paint garbage cans and new street numbers on the curbs; whitewash or paint a fence, shutters, a garage door, or a birdhouse; haul newspapers and cans to the recycling center; mail letters and deliver bill payments to neighborhood stores (saving postage for each one!).

You can also earn money by running errands, plant sitting, walking dogs, feeding cats and birds, babysitting, having a play group for the tots on the block . . . the list could go on and on!

To advertise your Outdoor Services, Inc., you could print some signs to put up around the neighborhood, ring doorbells, or drop handbills into mailboxes.

OUTDOOR SERVICES INC.

1. GRASS CUTTING
2. FENCE PAINTING
3. LEAF RAKING
4. NEWSPAPER HAULING
5. WALK YOUR DOG
6. BABY-SITTING
7. STACK FIREWOOD
8. CAR WASHING
9. FEED CATS
10. DELIVER THINGS

CALL -BILL- JENNY- LYNDA- MAX OR ROBIN

NEIGHBORHOOD ART FAIR

A neighborhood art fair can be a showcase for exhibiting all of the unusual and beautiful arts and crafts you've been making during the summer. Everyone can contribute something! Hang the sketches, paintings, photographs, sunprints, mobiles, pressed flowers and whatever else you have created on a wall, a fence, the side of a building, or from a tree or clothesline. Display the sculptures and nature crafts on small tables or covered boxes. Your huge papier mâché creations can be displayed right on the ground.

You can also turn your artistic talents into cash. Decide what you're willing to part with and put a price on it, but don't feel badly if your work doesn't sell; every budding artist has to begin somewhere. You can raise additional money by charging a small admission fee, selling tickets for a drawing, auctioning off a few "masterpieces," or selling homemade refreshments. You'll have no starving artists at this event!

Let everyone be a participant and join the neighborhood artists at work by staging an *art-in.* You'll need tables of basic supplies (crayons, paints and brushes, scissors, masking tape, glue, construction paper, cloth scraps, yarn, shells, feathers, etc.). Have everyone bring some of the supplies from home. Set out the makings for all kinds of easy projects, one to a table, with signs for nature crafts, puppets, jewelry, gadget printing, collages, mosaics, rubbings, and spatter painting. What else can you think up?

As an extra event at your art-in, work with a partner to create a *junk sculpture* using throwaway materials like boxes, egg cartons, containers of all sizes, tubes, Styrofoam trays and packing materials, toothpicks, corks, paper cups and plates, and anything else you can find. Give your sculpture a name and display it along with all the other "originals" at the art fair.

Ice Cream Social

A wonderful idea for a block party that includes all of the generations is an old-fashioned ice cream social. You might enjoy taking turns cranking the handle on an old ice-cream maker and feeling the change from a liquid to a thick, creamy mixture. Nowadays, though, you don't have to work so hard. Here's an easier way to whip up a batch, letting your mixer and freezer do it all.

This recipe makes just a pint, so unless you have a very large committee to make enough batches for the whole neighborhood, you might prefer to buy your ice cream in bulk. If so, everyone will have to pay his or her share.

Easy Ice Cream

YOU NEED:
3 mixing bowls
2 eggs
½ cup cream
2 tablespoons powdered sugar
flavorings

YOU DO:
1. Separate the eggs.
2. Beat the whites until thick and foamy.
3. In another bowl, beat the cream until thick and then carefully combine it with the beaten egg whites.
4. Add the sugar to the yolks, stirring until smooth.
5. Finally, mix everything together and add a small amount of flavoring (vanilla, lemon, orange, peppermint stick), cocoa, chocolate or carob chips, red hots, bits of fresh fruit (peaches, strawberries, etc.), nuts, or even peanut butter.
6. Pour into a freezer tray, bowl, or loaf pan and freeze for about an hour. Then scoop into balls and return to the freezer until you want to serve them in cones. Your ice cream cones will be added to the two billion that are sold in the United States each year!

Prepare bowls of toppings for do-it-yourself sundaes or banana splits. Include chopped nuts and sauces of all kinds, and, of course, whipped cream and a cherry to top off your ice cream delights. How about making hot fudge sundaes?

Hiland Withington Hall IX Easy Chocolate Sauce

YOU NEED:
4 squares unsweetened chocolate
1 cup milk
2 cups sugar

YOU DO:
Place all ingredients in a 2-quart saucepan and place over moderate heat. Stir occasionally until bubbles form. The sauce can be kept in a warmer over a candle. (This recipe makes enough sauce for 15–20 sundaes.)

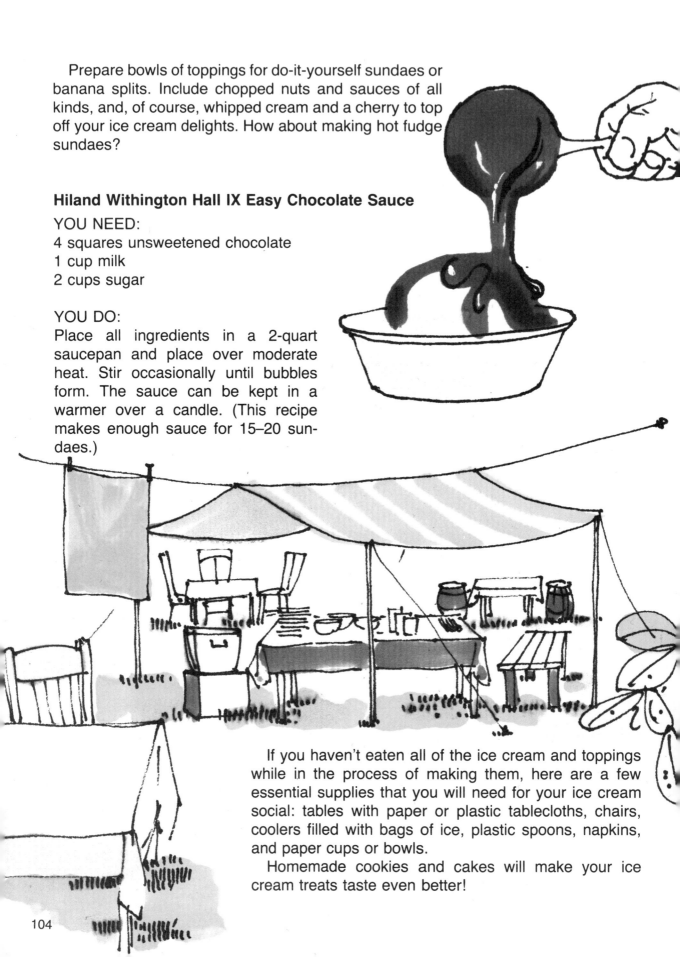

If you haven't eaten all of the ice cream and toppings while in the process of making them, here are a few essential supplies that you will need for your ice cream social: tables with paper or plastic tablecloths, chairs, coolers filled with bags of ice, plastic spoons, napkins, and paper cups or bowls.

Homemade cookies and cakes will make your ice cream treats taste even better!

Grandma and Grandpa's Trunk: Fashion Show of the Decades

An outdoor fashion show featuring outfits from bygone days is another great way to get the generations together and could provide amusing entertainment for your ice cream social as well!

Search your closets and attics (and your grandparents' and great-grandparents' too) for "dress-up clothes" that you can model. While you're rummaging through the trunks full of treasures, you may find a duster and goggles (used in the early open autos), spats (worn to protect shoes from the mud), and knickerbockers or "plus fours," bloomers, or middy blouses. Your efforts might produce an Al Capone fedora, a panama straw hat, or a Princess Eugénie hat (felt with a long feather), all popular in the early 1930s. Perhaps you'll even dig up some items that were in style at the turn of the century, like high-button shoes, stickpins, snuffboxes, or even a pince-nez.

When selecting your fashions, try to put together some clothes and accessories *from a particular decade.* For example, a 1950s ensemble would include penny loafers, bobbysox, a straight skirt, and a scarf tied around the neck (or tight jeans and a black leather jacket). Ask someone who grew up in the era you have chosen to help you write a description of your outfit for the announcer to read during your part in the show. These experts might even remember appropriate hair styles. Have you ever heard of a rat, a pompadour, or a chignon?

Use posters (perhaps decorated with cloth scraps, bits of fur, lace, or ribbons) to let the neighbors know what time to come to view the collections. Make signs on sandwich boards for the little kids in the neighborhood to wear during the show. Maybe some of the older generation would like to dress up and be models too!

To entertain during the intermission breaks, a barbershop quartet would certainly get everyone in the mood; or have a sing-along, inviting everyone to bring along a homemade instrument to accompany songs from each decade. Have you ever played a washboard, hummed through a comb, or used spoons for castanets? Wire-drum brushes make terrific sounds on paper. What could you find to make unusual music? Be inventive!

Capture this very special occasion by having a roving photographer on hand.

A photo-guessing contest would also be fun. Ask everyone ahead of time to lend you a snapshot taken when they were babies or young children. Mount all of the pictures on a large board, numbering each entry (being careful not to mark or bend the photos). Make a stack of answer sheets with blank lines numbered to match the picture board and have plenty of pencils available. Now try to guess who's who and award a prize for the most correct answers. Everyone should get at least one right!

106

Outdoor Theater

Here's an idea for any occasion where both the actors and the audience take part. No scenery and very few props are needed to make this backyard theater a success. The ground can be your stage, with a blanket tossed over a clothesline for the curtain. A box full of hats, scarves, wigs, glasses, masks, and other items will put your imaginations to work.

Try a variety of *theater games,* some using pantomime and others with both actions and words.

PROP BAG

Ask a group from the audience to sit in a semicircle. Then pass around a bag filled with silly props like a mustache, a bathing cap, an umbrella, or a whistle. Have each person, in turn, improvise part of a *continuous* story based on an item pulled from the bag.

ONE-WORD CHARADES

Each person or team has to act out *one* word, like *football, banana,* or *Monopoly,* by pantomiming or talking, being careful not to say that particular word.

STORY THEATER

Choose a famous story or fairytale and have people come up on stage to act out each part. As the story is read, they pantomime the characters' actions or ad lib the story, making up their lines as they go through the plot.

Stagecoach

In this version of story theater, the audience is divided into groups. They make special sound effects or do particular body movements every time a certain character appears or is mentioned during the play. For example, in a western saga, one group is assigned "clippity clop, clippity clop," to say or to clap in rhythm *every* time Cowboy Joe gallops onto the stage; another group hisses when the villain strides in; while a third group flaps their arms whenever a buzzard flies by. You can imagine the confusion when all of the characters appear at once!

CHANGING PLACES

One person begins by pretending to do an activity while everyone else watches. As soon as someone in the audience recognizes what the actor is doing, she steps into his place and continues the motions. For example, if an actor is pitching a tent, the next actor might carry on by pounding in the stakes or unrolling the sleeping bag.

Try this with several actors role playing different actions. Anyone from the audience can move into the roles and continue the pantomime. The original players then return to the audience to watch, until they are ready to change places again.

FAMILY SIT-COMS

Act out typical family situations by improvising everyday happenings: a dinner-table conversation; choosing which TV program to watch; planning a two-day trip and showing what happens in the car during the long second day; or deciding *who* should do *what* chores around the house. You'll discover some good role-playing situations here, and a lot of comedy too. Do you recognize your family in any of these "sit-com" scenes?

TRYOUTS

Stage some pretend tryouts for a well-known musical like *Grease* or *The Sound of Music.* Give each actor a piece of paper describing the type of charcter he or she is supposed to be. For example, loud and gruff; soft and sweet; nervous and fidgety; a stuck-up snob or clumsy clod. Two actors together "try out" for the parts, making up words and dancing to the familiar tunes. The audience then tries to guess what kinds of person they are portraying.

Country Fair

An ideal way to end the summer is to put on an old-time country fair for the whole neighborhood.

DISPLAYS AND CONTESTS

Brightly decorated tables and booths can display all kinds of summer products and projects: baskets of dried flowers; a pantry full of garden produce; nature crafts; creatures made from pumpkins, gourds, pinecones, nuts, and apples; cornhusk and corncob creations; artwork, including sculpture, tie-dye, batik, soap carvings, wood carvings, and photographs; and home-baked breads, rolls, cakes, and cookies.

As in real country fairs, sponsor contests and award prizes for homegrown items and handicrafts in various categories . . . the largest, the most beautiful or unusual, and so forth. A bake-off or a cupcake- and cookie-decorating contest will test the skills of the finest pastry chefs in the neighborhood. Think up contests such as watermelon, pizza, or pie eating; pumpkin decorating; glider and kite flying; hoop rolling; tug-o-war, blanketball, and other games and relay races.

TIE-DYE

FIRST BAKING

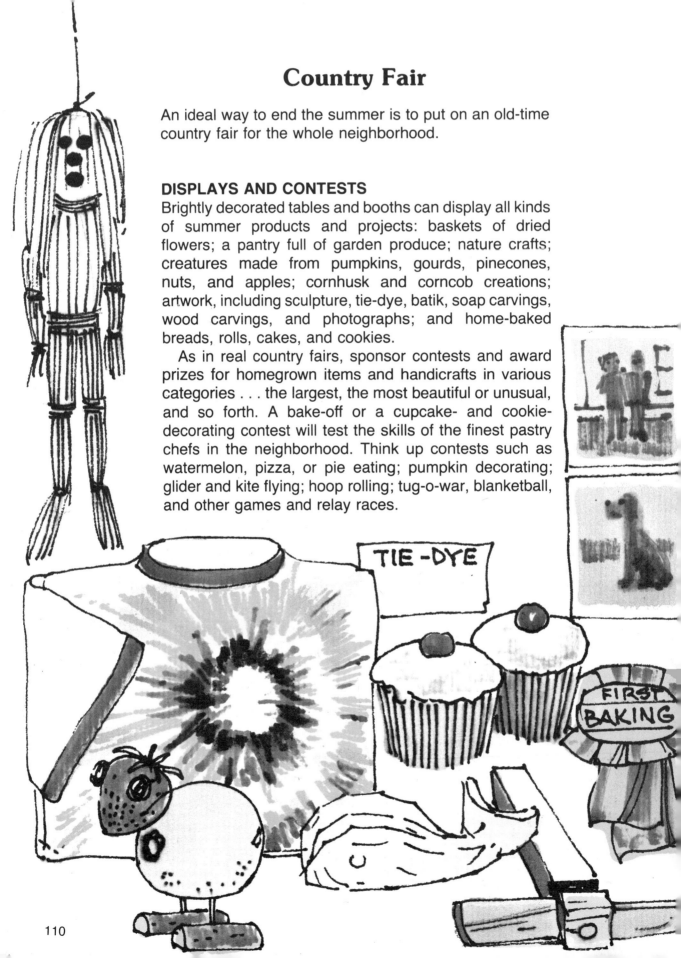

CARNIVAL GAMES

Who has ever heard of a country fair without a "midway" lined with carnival booths and rides? When setting up this attraction, certain items are a must: tickets, prizes, cold drinks, bakery goods, and, of course, a barker to attract the customers. Some ideas for booths are:

Roulette Wheel. Made from a cardboard pizza tray and hung on a tree, with each player placing a marker on a number chart while the "croupier" spins the arrow to determine the winning number.

Penny or Bean Bag Toss. Line up tin cans or boxes for targets.

Shuffleboard. Use hockey sticks and pucks (you can make your own by filling margarine tubs with sand), or brooms and bean bags. Draw the board on a sidewalk or driveway.

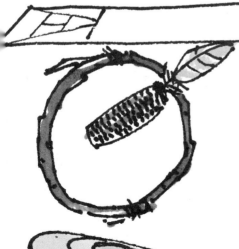

Indian Dart Throw. Poke a feather (real or paper) into a corncob and toss it through a hoop made from a bent twig.

Frisbee Throw. Sail paper plates or plastic Frisbees into a wastebasket or through a wire coat hanger or hula hoop.

Plate Smash. Collect chipped plates and cups from your neighbors, and line them up for the ball throwers in the crowd to demolish.

Sponge Squeeze. Using small pieces of sponge, see how long it takes to fill a tiny paper cup with water from a tub by soaking, squeezing, and squirting each drop.

Sponge Throwing. Particularly refreshing on a hot day (especially for the person whose head is the target!)

Ping-Pong Pond. Throw Ping-Pong balls into Styrofoam circles or margarine tubs floating in a large wading pool of water.

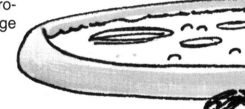

Bingo. Always a popular favorite!

Other games of skill include nail hammering (how fast can you pound a nail into a log?), balloon-burst (put on a blindfold and try to pop the balloon with a pin), balloon shaving (use shaving cream and bladeless razor), haystack hunt (look for hidden treasures), candle squirt-out—and don't forget some guessing games, a fortune teller, and perhaps even a magic show. Can you think of other booths or games of chance?

For the preschoolers: Younger children would enjoy rides in a wagon or cart or on a horse formed by two people inside a blanket; a make-up booth (lipstick, rouge, watercolor paints and brushes, and hats), or a make-your-own-jewelry booth (strings of colored macaroni, Play-Doh beads, dried corn, and melon seeds).

LIVESTOCK PET SHOW

Wouldn't you like to enter your cat, parakeet, or pet spider in a show much as 4-H kids exhibit the cows, lambs, and pigs they have raised themselves? Make an entry card for each pet and ribbons (blue, red, and white) for the winners.

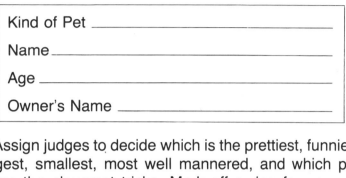

Kind of Pet _____

Name _____

Age _____

Owner's Name _____

Assign judges to decide which is the prettiest, funniest, largest, smallest, most well mannered, and which performs the cleverest tricks. Mark off a ring for your pet show using chalk on a paved area, or string and sticks for a grassy spot. Bring on the "livestock"!

As your country fair draws to a close, you may want to sell or *auction* off some of the handmade items that have been on display or have a *swap shop* to trade your own summer projects with those made by someone else. Finish the day with a box supper and ice cream social, and a good old-fashioned square dance. And then the next day—Good-bye, summer. Hello, school.

BIBLIOGRAPHY

CARPENTRY

Adkins, H. *Toolchest: A Primer of Woodcraft,* New York City: Walker and Co., 1973.

Brann, D. R. *How to Build Outdoor Furniture.* New York City: Directions Simplified, 1977.

Bright, J. *Outdoor Recreation Projects.* Farmington, Michigan: Structures Publishing Co., 1978.

Bubel, Nancy, and Mike Bubel. *Working Wood: A Guide for the Country Carpenter.* Emmaus, Pennsylvania: Rodale Press, 1977.

DeCristoforo, R. J. *Handtool Handbook for Woodworking.* Tucson: HP Books, 1977.

McPhee Gribble Publishers. *Carpentry.* Australia: Penguin Books, 1977.

Newman, T. R. *Woodcraft: Basic Concepts and Skills.* Radnor, Pennsylvania: Chilton Book Co., 1976.

Palmer, Bruce. *Making Children's Furniture and Playthings.* New York City: Workman Publishing, 1978.

Peterson, Franklynn. *Children's Toys You Can Build Yourself.* Englewood Cliffs, New Jersey: Prentice-Hall, Inc., 1978.

Simmons, John. *Carpentry Is Easy—When You Know How.* New York City: Arco Publishing, 1970.

Stiles, David. *The Tree House Book.* New York City: Avon, 1979.

Tangerman, E. J. *1001 Designs for Whittling and Wood Carving.* New York City: McGraw-Hill, 1976.

Todd, Leonard. *Trash Can Toys and Games.* New York City: Penguin Books, 1974.

Wilson, Jim. *Uncle Jim's Book of Things to Make.* Philadelphia, Pennsylvania: Running Press, 1976.

GAMES

Arnold, Arnold. *The World Book of Children's Games.* Garden City, New York: World Publishing Co., 1972.

Bentley, W. G. *Indoor and Outdoor Games.* Belmont, California: Fearon Publishers, 1966.

Ferretti, F. *The Great American Book of Sidewalk, Stoop, Dirt, Curb and Alley Games.* New York City: Workman Publishing, 1975.

Gallagher, Rachel. *Games in the Street.* New York City: Four Winds Press, 1977.

Grunfeld, Frederic. *Games of the World.* New York City: Holt, Rinehart and Winston, 1975.

Hall, J. Tillman. *Until the Whistle Blows.* Santa Monica: Goodyear Publishing Co., 1977.

Hockerman, Dennis. *Sidewalk Games.* Milwaukee: Raintree Children's Books, 1978.

Knapp, Herbert, and Mary Knapp. *One Potato, Two Potato.* New York City: Norton, 1976.

Langstaff, John, and Carol Langstaff. *Shimmy Shimmy Coke-Ca-Pop.* New York City: Doubleday and Co., 1973.

McLenighan, Valjean. *International Games.* Milwaukee: Raintree Children's Books, 1978.

Nelson, Esther L. *Movement Games for Children of All Ages.* New York City: Sterling Publishing Co., 1975.

O'Quinn, Garland, Jr. *Developmental Gymnastics.* Austin, Texas: University of Texas Press, 1977.

Resnick, Michael. *Gymnastics and You.* Chicago: Rand McNally, 1977.

Skolnik, Peter, *Jump Rope!* New York City: Workman Publishing, 1974.

Tatlow, Peter, *Gymnastics.* New York City: Atheneum, 1978.

Vinton, Iris. *Folkways Omnibus of Children's Games.* Harrisburg, Pennsylvania: Stackpole Books, 1970.

CRAFTS

Allen, Janet. *Exciting Things to Do with Nature Materials.* Philadelphia: J. B. Lippincott Co., 1977.

Blake, Jim, and Barbara Ernst. *The Great Perpetual Learning Machine.* Boston: Little, Brown and Co., 1976.

Caney, Steven. *Kids America.* New York City: Workman Publishing, 1978.

Cardozo, Peter, and Ted Menten. *The Second Whole Kids Catalogue.* New York City: Bantam Books, 1978.

————*The Whole Kids Catalogue.* New York City: Bantam Books, 1975.

Fiarotta, Phyllis. *Nostalgia Crafts Book.* New York City: Workman Publishing, 1975.

Hoople, Cheryl G. *The Heritage Sampler.* New York City: Dial Press, 1975.

Kinser, Charleen. *Outdoor Art for Kids.* Chicago: Follett Publishing, 1975.

Langford, Michel. *Starting Photography.* New York City: Hastings House, 1976.

LeFevre, Gregg. *Junk Sculpture.* New York City: Sterling Publishing Co., 1973.

McCoy, Ellin. *The Incredible Year-Round Playbook.* New York City: Random House, 1979.

Newsome, A. J. *Crafts and Toys from Around the World.* New York City: Messner Books, Simon and Schuster, 1972.

Pettit, Florence. *Whirligigs and Whimmy Diddles.* New York City: T. Y. Crowell, 1972.

Renner, A. G. *How to Build a Better Mousetrap Car and Other Experimental Science Fun.* New York City: Dodd, Mead, 1977.

Sattler, Helen. *Dollars From Dandelions* (101 Ways to Earn Money). New York City: Lothrop, Lee and Shepard, 1979.

Schnacke, Dick. *American Folk Toys: How To Make Them.* Baltimore: Penguin Books, 1974.

Simons, Robin. *Recyclopedia.* Boston: Houghton Mifflin Co., 1976.

Suid, Murray. *Painting with the Sun.* Boston: Dynamic Learning, 1973.

Vermeer, Jackie. *The Little Kid's Arts and Craft Book.* New York City: Taplinger Publishing Co., 1975.

Weiss, Harvey. *Beginning Artist's Library.* Reading, Massachusetts: Addison-Wesley Publishing Co., 1978.

Wiseman, Ann. *Making Things I* and *Making Things II.* Boston: Little, Brown and Co., 1974, 1975.

NATURE

Blough, Glenn. *Bird Watchers and Bird Feeders.* New York: McGraw Hill, 1963.

Bowden, A. O. *Wild Green Things in the City.* New York City: T. Y. Crowell, 1972.

Caras, Roger. *A Zoo in Your Room.* New York City: Harcourt Brace Jovanovich, 1975.

Chinery, M. *Enjoying Nature with Your Family.* New York City: Crown Publishing, 1977.

Clark, Collins and Collins. *The Naturalist—Nature Walk.* Provo, Utah: Press Publishing, 1972.

————*The Naturalist—Botanical Art.* Provo, Utah: Press Publishing, 1972.

Cosgrove, Irene. *My Recipes Are for the Birds.* New York City: Doubleday and Co., 1975.

Dowden, A. O. *The Blossom on the Bough: A Book of Trees.* New York City: T. Y. Crowell, 1975.

Edwards, Joan. *Caring for Trees on City Streets.* New York City: Charles Scribner and Sons, 1975.

Frankel, Lillian, and Godfrey Frankel. *101 Best Nature Games and Projects.* New York City: Gramercy Publishing Co., 1969.

Freedman, Russell. *How Birds Fly.* New York City: Holiday, 1977.

Garelick, May. *It's About Birds.* New York City: Holt, Rinehart and Winston, 1978.

Hussey, Lois, and Catherine Pacino. *Collecting for the City Naturalists.* New York City: T. Y. Crowell, 1972.

GARDENING

Barrett, Patricia, and Rosemary Dalton. *The Kid's Garden Book.* Concord, California: Nitty Gritty Productions, 1974.

Eckstein, Joan, and Joyce Gleit. *Fun with Growing Things.* New York City: Avon Books, 1975.

Paul, Aileen. *Kid's Outdoor Gardening.* Garden City, New York: Doubleday, 1978.

Schaeffer, Elizabeth. *Dandelion, Pokeweed and Goosefoot.* Reading, Massachusetts: Addison-Wesley, 1978.

Selsam and Hunt. *A First Look at the World of Plants.* New York City: Walker and Co., 1978.

Skelsey, Alice, and Gloria Huckaby. *Growing Up Green.* New York City: Workman Publishing, 1973.

Surcouf, Lorraine. *Growing a Green Thumb.* New York City: Workman Publishing, 1975.

CAMPING OUT

Allison, L. *Sierra Club Summer Book.* New York City: Charles Scribner's Sons, 1977.

Broder, Bill. *1979 Sierra Club Calendar and Almanac for Young People.* New York City: Sierra Club Charles Scribner's Sons, 1978.

Paul, Aileen. *Kids Camping.* New York City: Doubleday and Co., 1973.

Thomas, Dian. *Roughing It Easy I and II.* Provo, Utah: Brigham Young University Press, 1974, 1975.

COOKING

Abisch, Roz, and Boche Kaplian. *The Munchy, Crunchy Healthy Kid's Snack Book.* New York City: Walker and Co., 1976.

Cadwallader, A. *The Whole Earth Cook Book.* New York City: Bantam Books, 1972.

————*Cooking Adventures for Kids.* Boston: Houghton Mifflin Co., 1974.

Cooper, Jane. *Love at First Bite.* New York City: Alfred A. Knopf, 1977.

Cross, Margaret, and Jean Fiske. *Backpacker's Cookbook.* Berkeley, California: Ten Speed Press, 1974.

Feig, B. K. *Now You're Cooking.* Chicago: J. B. Pal and Co., 1975.

Glovach, Linda. *Potions, Lotions, Tonics and Teas.* Englewood Cliffs, New Jersey: Prentice-Hall, 1977.

McClenahan, P. *Cool Cooking for Kids.* Belmont, California: Fearon Publishers, 1976.

Mohney, R. *Trailside Cooking.* Harrisburg, Pennsylvania: Stackpole Books, 1976.

Paul, Aileen. *Kids Cooking.* New York City: Doubleday, 1970.